How Do I Live for God?

**Books in the Life-Transforming Truths
from a Never-Changing God Series**
Book 1: *What Is God Like?*
Book 2: *How Do I Get to Know God?*
Book 3: *How Do I Live for God?*

Other Books by D. James Kennedy
Abortion: Cry of Reality
Beginning Again
Chain Reaction
*Character and Destiny: A Nation in
    Search of Its Soul*
Defending the First Amendment
*Delighting God: How to Live
    at the Center of God's Will*
Education: Public Problems, Private Solutions
Evangelism Explosion
The God of Great Surprises
The Great Deception
Help God, I Hurt!
Highway to Holiness
Knowing God's Will
Learning to Live with the People You Love
Messiah: Prophecies Fulfilled
Nation in Shame
Real Meaning of the Zodiac
Reconstruction
Spiritual Renewal
This Is the Life
Truth and Education
Truths That Transform
Turn It to Gold
What If Jesus Had Never Been Born?
Why I Believe
Wolves Among Us
Your Prodigal Child: Help for Hurting Parents

How Do I Live for God?

Life-Transforming Truths from a Never-Changing God

Book 3

D. James Kennedy

Fleming H. Revell
A Division of Baker Book House Co
Grand Rapids, Michigan 49516

Published by Fleming H. Revell
a division of Baker Book House Company
P.O. Box 6287, Grand Rapids, MI 49516-6287

Printed in the United States of America

Library of Congress Cataloging-in-Publication Data

Kennedy, D. James (Dennis James), 1930–
    Life-transforming truths from a never-changing God /
D. James Kennedy.
      p. cm.
    ISBN 0-8007-5558-8 (bk. 1)
    ISBN 0-8007-5557-X (bk. 2)
    ISBN 0-8007-5559-6 (bk. 3)
    Contents: bk. 1. What is God Like? — bk. 2. How do I
get to know God? — bk. 3. How do I live for God?
    1. Theology, Doctrinal—Popular works. 2. Christian
life. 3. Westminster Confession of Faith. 4.
Fundamentalist churches—Doctrines. I. Title.
[BT77.K2767   1995]
230'.044—dc20   94-179918

Contents

Introduction

I remember a time when I thought that if ever I really let God get hold of my life he would, no doubt, make me miserable. I was not a new believer at the time. Actually I was in seminary studying to be a minister.

I had heard a preacher say, "If you really believe God, you surrender yourself to his hands. Just step out in faith and he will lead you. If God wants you to be a missionary he will lead you. If he does not he will close the door. Do you believe that?"

"Yes," I said in my heart, "I believe that."

"Then sign up!" he continued.

"Yes," I said in my heart, "I should sign up."

He was talking about signing up to go to the Belgian Congo. To this day I do not know why I went to the mission board to sign up to go to the Belgian Congo. I did not want to go to the Belgian Congo. I did not feel called to go to the Belgian Congo. But I was going to do what this fellow said. I then learned that in the middle of the Belgian Congo was the world's largest leper colony. I had had a life-long phobia about leprosy, and I was convinced that if ever I came within 100 miles of the disease I would be stricken. Now I was probably going to be plopped right down into the middle of a leper colony. Soon I would be one little quivering lump, sans toes, sans feet, sans hands, sans all the rest of me.

This was ridiculous. Why was I working myself into such a state? Now I think I understand myself and my enemy a little better. Satan had been telling me that God was mean, and now he was really going to fix me because he had me right in the palm of his hand to do whatever he wanted.

God's good, transforming will

You can imagine what the Lord did with my uncalled "call" to the Belgian Congo. He tossed me out on my ear and slammed that door hard. God said, "I need you in the Congo like I need a hole in the head. With your neuroses you wouldn't last six months." Instead he plopped me down in Fort Lauderdale, Florida, which he knew I could handle a lot better. I learned a great truth about the will of God for my life—God is good, and what he wants is good for me.

This is the third book in a trilogy about the life-transforming doctrines of Christian faith. Book 1 looked at what we believe about God as Father, Son, and Holy Spirit—a quest up the life-transforming mountain of the understanding of the Creator and the creature. Book 2 answered basic questions about salvation—why Christ had to die to save us, how God's grace works in our lives to save us, and how God continues to change us through sanctification. We finished with a look at assurances the believer has for an eternal life to come. We now look more closely at the Christian life itself. If all the Bible teaches about God and the gospel is true, what should I do? The answer starts again in God and the Holy Spirit's residence within the heart. It involves all that we think, say, and do—our worldview, ethics, worship, citizenship, relationships. It involves where we think history is heading, so we will make some observations about how Christians should live as they await the culmination of history in Christ's return and judgment.

As in books 1 and 2, our guidebook for this tour of transforming Bible precepts will be the *Westminster Confession of Faith* and the *Westminster Larger* and *Shorter* catechisms. I chose to follow these statements, not because they are inspired, but because they closely reflect what the Bible teaches and are clear, uncompromising statements of faith and life. These documents were written in the midst of national spiritual crisis, the English Civil War of the 1640s. I believe they offer keen insights for our own day of spiritual and cultural crisis. Ours is an era of malnourished church members who have been spoonfed tapioca and cheesecake religion until their spiritual stomachs are bloated and their hearts are clogged with the cholesterol of meaningless "I wanna be me" self-fulfillment.

One preacher commented that the church began its life conquering Roman idolatry and seems to be losing the battle to survive "egolatry." Paul told Timothy,

> This know also, that in the last days perilous times shall come. For men shall be lovers of their own selves, covetous, boasters, proud, blasphemers, disobedient to parents, unthankful, unholy, without natural affection, truce-breakers, false accusers, incontinent, fierce, despisers of those that are good, traitors, heady, highminded, lovers of pleasure more than lovers of God; having a form of godliness, but denying the power thereof: from such turn away. [2 Timothy 3:1–5]

That sounds like such a shopping list of the ills of our day that one wonders how "last" these days are. I don't know. I do think it noteworthy that Paul told Timothy not to have anything to do with such people, so they must have been around even in the first century!

The world-infected church of the last days has been around a long time. But now it has reached a state where a minority of preachers and teachers faithfully impart life-transforming scriptural doctrines. The drift away from biblical truth in the Western European and North American churches began long ago, and generations have been born, lived, and gone into eternity without even a rudimentary understanding of the life-transforming teachings. If everything in these books is old news, wonderful! Rejoice as you meditate on their meaning with me. If this is new news, that also is wonderful. I delight to share these truths with someone hearing them for the first time.

Thy will be done

Each of these three books has a theme idea that helps organize, at least in my mind, the topics covered. Book 1 searched out the path of quest toward knowing God. Book 2 looked at the Christ of our salvation who "makes all things new." Now we turn to the words of Jesus as he prayed in a garden, facing the worst trial any human being ever faced. His prayer: *"Not my will, but thine, be done"* (Matthew 26:39; Mark 14:36; Luke 22:42).

To live a victorious life we must believe that God is good and that his will for our lives is excellent. We know well his will for humanity: to repent and believe. The Lord God advises post-modern twenty-first century Western culture as he advised the prophet Jeremiah's generation—that we stand at the crossroads and must consider carefully the road to take:

Stand at the crossroads and look;
    ask for the ancient paths,
ask where the good way is, and walk in it,
    and you will find rest for your souls. [Jeremiah 6:16
NIV]

We are to "glorify God and enjoy him forever." The prophet Micah observed what that means in the day-to-day nitty-gritty of life:

Wherewith shall I come before the LORD, and bow myself before the high God? shall I come before him with burnt offerings, with calves of a year old? Will the LORD be pleased with thousands of rams, or with ten thousands of rivers of oil? shall I give my firstborn for my transgression, the fruit of my body for the sin of my soul? He hath shewed thee, O man, what is good; and what doth the LORD require of thee, but to do justly, and to love mercy, and to walk humbly with thy God? [Micah 6:6–8]

But God also has a unique and excellent will for each of his children, for those who have come to Christ to be Savior and Lord. Christians will only come to believe that God's will for us is excellent, however, to the extent that we place our hands, our lives, in the hands of God—the hands that are pierced for us. Those words of Jesus, "Not my will but thine be done," make us want to start back in horror and terror. Surely there is a Congo leper colony hiding within. But God has not called *us* to be the savior of the world. That job is taken. Rather, we are called simply to follow the God who loves us with an everlasting love.

We must also believe that God is wise. Our parents did what they thought best for us, and often they fouled it all up. How many parents have tried to make foot-ball players out of poets or physicians out of football players? As a parent I know that a superabundance of ignorance resides within us. But think about what we learned about the wisdom and omniscience of God. Now think about how foolish our way, plans, and desires can be. Honestly, who do we really want calling the shots? If we could comprehend the wisdom of God and the goodness of God, we would say, "Into those hands let me cast my life." God's plan for every sphere of life is vastly better than any that our paltry minds can devise.

Meaning for a meaningless world

Vanity of vanities, saith the Preacher, vanity of vanities; all is vanity. [Ecclesiastes 1:2]

Ecclesiastes is an odd book of Scripture, for in it King Solomon (the wise Teacher) discusses at length the meaning of life lived in the will of the human individual. Only occasionally, slipping in around the edge, does he refer to God's will for life. Then at the end of the book he throws open the door and proclaims that only God's will offers any meaning at all for the inhabitant on planet earth.

Solomon tells us that he had sampled life from all sides, and he also perhaps met some of the same types of people I have encountered in thirty-five years of ministry. Solomon finds that each kind of person has one of only two centers of consciousness and desire.

One type of person is worldly-wise or "street smart." This person has it all together, or seems to. Solomon was one of these himself, a Renaissance man who studied and pondered and became wise in the ways of life, self-sufficient and knowledgeable in many disciplines. As the wizard of the land of Oz gave to the scarecrow,

Solomon had a doctorate in thinkology. But what he learned with his wisdom was that "what is twisted cannot be straightened; what is lacking cannot be counted" (1:15 NIV). Looking for satisfaction only in knowledge, the worldly philosopher said, "My will be done." But all he learned was how bad off he was. It was a "chasing after the wind" without eternal meaning. In modern philosophical terms Solomon relates that looking to self for wisdom leads only to nihilism.

The second kind of person Solomon introduces has a life focused on self-fulfillment. This is the child of our age, who believes we only go around once in life, so we must grab all the fun we can. We work hard to get ahead, so we deserve the best. Sensual desires rule. "My will be done." The person centered in self-fulfillment strongly believes in being what secular humanist psychology calls "self-actualized." If this person makes any sort of profession for God at all it is a religion built upon emotion and "what the church can do for me and mine." This person, if awareness of sin enters into the picture at all, considers that at least 51 percent of goodness will be enough to satisfy God, who is loving and wouldn't really send anyone to hell anyway. Yet hell is where this person is bound, and all the grasping selfishness of this lifestyle will not buy happiness or contentment in the meantime. This is of all lives the most wasted.

Akin to the one interested only in self-fulfilled desires is the third person—one who desires to collect as much wealth as possible. Work becomes an obsession and the wealth in a stock portfolio the barometer of success. Through money, "My will be done." But Solomon warns us that

> He that loveth silver shall not be satisfied with silver; nor he that loveth abundance with increase: this is also

vanity. When goods increase, they are increased that eat them: and what good is there to the owners thereof, saving the beholding of them with their eyes? [5:10–11]

A fourth kind of person seems far different, yet perhaps not so different. This person centers life in altruism. This person lives a harried and outwardly fulfilling career of serving others. At the root is a strong sense of works righteousness that may hide feelings of guilt and worthlessness and inadequacy. Certainly such a life is good enough and worthwhile. But alas, for all the sweat, blood, and tears expended in the name of human betterment, this person seems unsatisfied and embittered by it all, sarcastically saying there is "one upright man among a thousand, but not one upright woman among them all" (7:28 NIV). The righteous get what the wicked deserve, and the wicked what the upright deserve, so that there is no justice anywhere (8:14). Amazingly enough, students of human behavior say that the altruist rarely comes to the land of contentment. Self-sacrifice will not bring grace. Grace, rather than justice, is what this person is working so hard to find. In his or her heart the focus still is on self and desires. "My will be done." This is a life of work and worry but not of worth.

There are other kinds of people we might name; Solomon mentions a few others in passing, all of whom are assigned the same fate—meaninglessness, arising from the cry, "My will be done!"

Finally, in Ecclesiastes 12 the teacher drops the other shoe. Yes, there is meaning in life, but only for the one who says, "*Thy* will be done." Don't wait to find meaning in life, Solomon counsels us:

Remember now thy Creator in the days of thy youth, while the evil days come not, nor the years draw nigh, when thou shalt say, I have no pleasure in them. [12:1]

The Hebrew word for "remember" is an interesting one; it means "to act decisively for." To act decisively for God, Solomon goes on to say, is the only way to find eternal significance:

> Let us hear the conclusion of the whole matter: Fear God, and keep his commandments: for this is the whole duty of man. [12:13]

What is the chief purpose of humanity but to glorify God and to enjoy him forever? Only in Jesus Christ is that possible, for only Jesus Christ moves the center of consciousness from self to God's will—a good and perfect will.

What makes an ethical standard "Christian"?

What is the moral law? The moral law is the declaration of the will of God to mankind, directing and binding every one to personal, perfect, and perpetual conformity and obedience thereunto, in the frame and disposition of the whole man, soul and body, and in the performance of all those duties of holiness and righteousness which he oweth to God and man: promising life upon the fulfilling, and threatening death upon the breach of it. [Westminster Larger Catechism, question 93]

1

The Cut-Flower Generation

hen you know what God has done in Christ, you will know what you ought to do," said the eminent Scottish Christian leader James Stewart.

If this is true, then Christians should, above all others, know what they ought to do. Christians alone have experienced firsthand what God has done in Christ.

That experience of coming to Christ—of being justified, adopted, and sanctified by the grace of God—is the foundation for a life-transforming way of living. It is an ethic that fulfils our primary reason for existing—*to glorify God and enjoy him forever*. By now most readers are familiar with the question and answer from the *Westminster Shorter Catechism*: "What is the chief end of man? Man's chief end is to glorify God and enjoy him forever." We have looked at the God we are called to glorify and enjoy and at God's plan of salvation in Jesus Christ. Because Christ stepped into our shoes and took on himself our sin, we can have a relationship with the God we are called to glorify and enjoy.

So now the Christian man and woman stand in the presence of God. The Christian can call the Father *Abba*—Daddy! The Christian knows that the penalty for breaking the law of God no longer hangs over his or her head like a sentence of death. Such love from

God deserves a fitting response from the one who is called to glorify and enjoy.

So how do we live for God today? Three resources stand at our disposal, and this book is about those great gifts God has provided to the one who is called to glorify and enjoy:

1. *We have newness.* We just aren't the same fallen creatures who were lost in rebellion against God; who were not able to fulfil God's purpose. We no longer are under the curse of the lawbreaker. We are a new creation, a re-creation. We still sin, but we have new options.

2. *We have an ethical system that works.* No way of living ever devised by the human mind can fulfil God's purpose for humanity. That wasn't why these ethical systems came into being, so they simply cannot meet the need. Ours was designed by the Designer of all things. He revealed it to us in the Bible. It is compatible with how we are made.

> *The heart is deceitful above all things, and desperately wicked: who can know it? I the LORD search the heart, I try the reins, even to give every man according to his ways, and according to the fruit of his doings.*
> [Jeremiah 17:9–10]

3. *We have God's presence within us.* The Holy Spirit now pervades the Christian's being. God the Holy Spirit lives in the heart of every Christian, revealing God and empowering us to glorify and enjoy him.

A lifestyle of newness

The *Westminster Confession,* in its statement on the law of God (chapter 19) is helpful for understanding what it means to have a lifestyle of newness. First, God gave to Adam a promise or covenant of life. This covenant had two provisions. If Adam obeyed God's one rule, he and his children would live in close relation with God forever. If Adam disobeyed, broken relationship and death would result. Second, after Adam disobeyed, God unveiled a new covenant of grace and a more detailed set of laws so men and women would know how to live. These covenantal laws find their most basic expression in the ten commandments—ten principles explaining our duty toward God (the first four commandments) and our duty toward one another (commandments five through ten). Other laws were given to the nation of Israel as God's covenant people, to guide their worship and actions. All of these laws provided principles for understanding God and his will, they restrained the evil in fallen humanity, and they pointed toward the final answer for sin, Jesus Christ.

Third, God's law still stands as a set of principles, which are summarized in the law of love, what Jesus said are the greatest commandments: "Thou shalt love the Lord thy God with all thy heart, and with all thy soul, and with all thy mind. . . . Thou shalt love thy neighbor as thyself" (Matthew 22:37–39; see Deuteronomy 6:5 and Leviticus 19:18). Explains Galatians 5:6:

"For in Jesus Christ neither circumcision availeth any thing, nor uncircumcision [the keeping of the law of the Jews or the Gentiles]; but faith which worketh by love."

So the law of God is useless, right? Hardly, according to the *Westminster Confession*:

> Although true believers be not under the law as a covenant of works, to be thereby justified or condemned; yet is it of great use to them, as well as to others; in that, as a rule of life, informing them of the will of God and their duty, it directs and binds them to walk accordingly.

The law informs Christians of the will of God and "binds them to walk accordingly," not out of fear but out of faith, expressing itself through love. It shows how far the believer's actual behavior is from God's ideal and so restrains the evil that remains in the heart of any human being. Its threats show us how God feels about sin; its promises show how he desires obedience. It encourages a closer walk with God.

Fourth, such purposes are God's grace to us. Once the law promised only death; but now it helps us live our new life.

The *ought* and the *is*

Without fear of contradiction I will relate that the Christian ethical system is the only system that really works, if by "working" we mean a system that brings justice and peace to a world in the throes of pain, discontent, dissatisfaction, and meaninglessness. First, it has a source of power in the Holy Spirit that is not found in any other ethic. Second, it works through love, rather than fear. Third, it is built upon the revealed will of God, the Master Architect of life and the Giver of its meaning.

"Ours is a cut-flower civilization," said Elton Trueblood. He explained that a cut-flower civilization has much beauty—its technological advances are stirring; its quality of life is unequaled for the availability of luxury and ease; its thought is capable of great literature and magnificent art. But this momentary beauty hides the fact that the society is terminal. Civilization is cut off from the source of its life and is inevitably decaying. Surely no one in the know can miss seeing the wilt of the petals and the droop and drop of the leaves. Our state is one of advanced degeneration.

This moral crisis is unlike any the world has ever before known, remarks Will Herberg, graduate professor of philosophy and culture at Drew University in an article, "What is the Moral Crisis of Our Time?" Herberg describes this crisis as fundamentally different from the crises of war or riots or crime. "The trouble seems to come, not from the breaking of moral laws, but from something far more serious—the rejection of the conception that there is any moral law at all." We live in what is, to a great extent today, an amoral society.

What is ethics anyway? First of all, note that ethics does not declare what *is*. It declares what *ought to be*. It enunciates norms or standards of conduct. It condemns, condones, or commends. It makes *value judgments;* therein lies the rub.

Everyone has some sort of value system, an ethical framework on which the person builds and lives. So deep within us that we hardly know they are there lie presumptions and assumptions about what we "know" to be true and good. These assumptions color virtually everything we see and hear. Now those perceptions seem to be colored by the assumption that no action is always, under every circumstance, right or wrong. No course of action is morally superior to all others. This assumption lies at the heart of the moral revolution of our time.

Rules for the game

Secular ethics is speculative. It must speculate or rationalize what courses of action are right for human beings to follow because no master plan set of rules is recognized. One of the most influential secular ethical systems has drastically influenced the late twentieth-century church. This system is called situational ethics. The situation ethics movement is no longer a major force, but its ideas remain entrenched. Joseph Fletcher coined the term *situational ethics* and based it upon the philosophy that there can be no absolute set of rights and wrongs. What is important is to show love to other people. Whatever is the most loving response in a particular situation is right. H. Richard Niebuhr applied this to Christian conduct in a church that no longer believed in absolutes or a divinely revealed Scripture. Niebuhr said that morality should be built upon love for God. But how does one know how to love God in a given situation, for the Bible is no longer to be believed. We must speculate. T. Ralph Morton, a proponent of this "new morality," admitted it makes "Christ-centered" decision-making more complex:

> Even to speak of "exceptions" is to presuppose that there are "rules" laid down somewhere, and it is here that the Protestant Christian, seeking to come to a Christian decision, is at his greatest loss; there simply

are no commonly accepted rules in Protestantism for making ethical decisions.

How then does a Christian know what behavior is Christ-centered? What the Bible said Christ himself did is irrelevant, because that was another time and set of situations, and it is not real history anyway. Rather, we know what to do when we see what God is doing in a situation and act accordingly. Niebuhr said the decisive ethical question to ask is, "What is happening?" and then find the fitting response.

What a remarkable admission. God has no definite pattern of behavior, no goal, no law. We are simply winging it. Nothing is revealed.We have joined the team in the middle of the game, and no one can tell us what game we are playing or its rules. We must go out on the field, imagine what is the loving thing to do, and just make up the rules as we go along, according to what seems right. It is all subjective and open to the interpretation of the moment. The prophet Jeremiah sneered at the individual's ability to come up with an ethic without help:

> The heart is deceitful above all things, and desperately wicked: who can know it? I the LORD search the heart, I try the reins, even to give every man according to his ways, and according to the fruit of his doings. [Jeremiah 17:9–10]

Absolutely no absolutes

Without any light to guide their speculations, secular ethicists disagree wildly among themselves. There is only one point on which these systems agree: There is absolutely no absolute standard of morality for all people everywhere. Many times I have heard critics of the Christian principles of conduct remonstrate that some element of the biblical ethical system seems unwarranted, confining, or oppressive. One thing that might do all these complainers some good is to take a very close look at secular ethics and see the infinite gulf that separates the best efforts of the secularist from Christian ethics.

It only takes a quick survey of ethical systems devised by the ethical speculators to see that all have elements of truth, with a large admixture of error. Satan rarely uses the total lie as his tool. He blends truth and falsehood—a little bait on the hook.

Consequences

Who lived an ethically superior life? Florence Nightingale? Al Capone? Nero? The apostle Paul? Without an absolute standard there is no possible way to prove that any of these people is superior ethically to any other. That applies to mass murderers and despots. Is it better to save life or to take life? Can a massacre be ethically good or bad? There are large numbers of people who might take either side of such questions, at least under some circumstances. Ethical systems have advocated genocide, infanticide, abortion, and mercy killing. What good, then, is any ethical system at all?

Usually no good at all. To qualify as an ethical system a philosophy must attach itself to one of the three parts that are involved in any human deed:

1. the *motive* that lies behind the act;
2. the *act* itself;
3. the *results* or consequences of the act.

Most ethical systems focus on the third aspect—the end to which a deed is directed, or its consequence.

These systems of ethics are *teleological*, from the Greek word *telos*, meaning "end." Teleological ethics establish right or wrong by seeing if the end justifies the means. How do you know whether the end is worthwhile? That all depends on your perspective. If no God has revealed himself, the most powerful person has the most important perspective and sets the ethical agenda.

So what kinds of teleological ethical systems have been devised? One of the oldest and most common is *egoism*, from the Greek word *ego*, meaning "I." Egoism is straightforward: What is ultimately good (called the *summum bonum*) is whatever is ultimately good for me. I decide how to act by determining which course of action will do me the most good or the least harm. If that seems selfish, remember that no one has ever demonstrated that genocide or torture is wrong. A little old-fashioned selfishness should not bother us. To say selfishness is "wrong" is to lean on Christian standards, with absolutes of right or wrong. Such value judgments are quaintly irrelevant or even harmful for social evolution.

In her book *The Virtue of Selfishness*, Ayn Rand argues that the only ethical system worth following is egoism, or "enlightened selfishness." As an atheist, Rand believes that most of the world's problems are caused by muddle-headed altruists who are trying to do something for somebody else. How much better if everybody would just take care of "number-one." A selfish society would want to make the streets safe, would want to deal with social problems that might erupt into class warfare, would want to progress in technology to make life easier and more enjoyable, would want good marriages and family relationships, since those make life more bearable, and would want world peace. This does seem a sensible program, even from purely selfish motivations. If we condemn egoism out-of-hand are we saying it is right for an individual to seek his or her own ultimate harm? One definition of insanity is that the person lacks concern for his or her own well-being. Why wouldn't enlightened selfishness make the world a utopia? Or perhaps we should ask why egoism has not led to such fine things, since that is the philosophy under which most of our own society operates. There must be a flaw somewhere.

A second teleological system of ethics was originated in the 1800s by Jeremy Bentham and popularized by the famed philosopher and essayist John Stuart Mill. *Utilitarianism* adopts the principle of utility—an act is only as good as its benefit for larger society. Here the focus is not on the individual but on humankind. This sounds much better than egoism as a way of life, especially when we hear the utilitarian maxim: *"The greatest good for the greatest number."* That seems a fine way to live, and many governments operate on this principle. Utilitarianism is the value system of evolution. The greatest good for the greatest number is the good that advances the species. If someone is sick, has bad genes, or is deformed, the greatest good for the greatest number is for the person to die. Such is the mind-set behind genetic testing—the goal to make humanity better and better. Eugenics, a system of trying to weed out the racially or culturally inferior stock, grew out of this ethical system early in the 1900s. Planned Parenthood was founded on eugenic principles. The most famous experiment in utilitarian eugenics was in Germany in the 1930s and 1940s. If 90 million blond, Nordic, blue-eyed Aryans are developing a super-race, and a few million miserable Jews are fouling up the gene pool, then what could be more virtuous than to exterminate them? If the greatest good for all future people of the world is the destruction of every European Jew, East European gypsy, mentally or physically impaired person, and subversive Christian, then this destruction is the *summum bonum*. Utilitarianism also is the basic ethical system underlying communism. The end is the good, and the end is the communist society. Is murder right or wrong? That depends on whether it advances the communist state. So 15 million Ukrainians, 40 million Chinese, and 20 or 30 million Russians are killed. What is that compared to the infinite bliss of a future paradisiacal world?

The apostle Paul headed off utilitarian religion when he foresaw this response to the gospel of grace in Jesus Christ: "God's grace is a wonderful thing. I want more and more of it. And I get more grace when God forgives my sin. Therefore, it is good to sin, since that unleashes grace." Imagining such a response nearly gave the apostle apoplexy:

> What then? shall we sin, because we are not under the law, but under grace? God forbid. Know ye not, that to whom ye yield yourselves servants to obey, his servants ye are to whom ye obey; whether of sin unto death, or of obedience unto righteousness? [Romans 6:15–16]

This sounds like total rejection of teleological thinking. But another teleological ethic outwardly looks very like the sort of ethic Paul himself describes, the system of *altruism*. Altruism says that the only thing I must consider is my neighbor's well-being— the individual with whom I happen to be dealing. I will decide not to follow my own desires. In fact, I will go out of my way to reject my own interests if my actions will help another human being. How gracious this sounds, but on what basis am I to deny myself? This may cover a great act of philanthropy or the self-sacrifice of throwing one's body on a hand grenade to save one's buddies, but it breaks down in daily reality, which is, after all, where most ethical decisions are made.

Altruistic ideals must have an object more definite than "humanity" to be a basis for life. Why should I consider the well-being of my brother rather than my own? In an evolutionary worldview there is absolutely no reason at all, for neither my brother nor sister nor I have eternal value. The only value is in momentary well-being. I may get a good feeling inside when I give of my substance to make another's lot more bearable. But even this satisfaction must be tinged with bittersweet. For if I sacrifice so that someone is fed today, the person is nothing more than an animal who will have other needs tomorrow and next week and on and on until death. My act of kindness does no more than to stave off the inevitable, so why bother? It is, as Solomon saw, a chasing after the wind. King Louis XIV of France put his finger on the flaw with altruism in his line: "After me, the deluge!" In other words, why should I care about the human race? I'll have my fun, and then let the rains come.

Pragmatism presents another ethical option. The maxim of the pragmatist is: "You can't fight success!" Whatever works is right. By this concept many govern their lives, yet how does one build a life on this pattern? How does one know, when making a decision, whether one course of action is going to work, and another is not? The pragmatist, therefore, must build an ethical system upon experience and statistical probability. Something has worked, so likely it will work now. But if it has worked nine times out of ten and we are the tenth, the statistics may spell disaster. Also, how well do we know all the consequences of past actions? Perhaps a decision has not worked as well as we think. The pragmatic way provides no certain guide for humanity because ends do not justify the means.

Motives

If the result is not the proper test for an ethical system, then what about the motive? A number of philosophers have said, correctly, that we cannot rationally compute what the results of an act will be. The important thing is just to act, for by acting in any way we attest that we are alive and acting upon our environment—we prove that we exist. So this philosophy came to be called *existentialism*. While teleological ethics is subjective without admitting it, existentialism brags about its subjective decision-making. Its maxim is the bumper-sticker proverb: "If it feels good, do it." Its theme song is: "There's no tomorrow. Tonight's the night for love."

For obvious reasons this became a popular ethical response, and at least it is more honest than teleological ethics. The existentialist sees no absolute pattern for ethics, admits it, and glories in it. But its result is the same: If I can equally display my existence by helping a little old lady across the street and by kicking her brains in, the ethical system is not very helpful.

We already introduced the variation of altruism in situational ethics, which also deals with motives. We have no ultimate standards, no laws from God but that we love one another. Look at the situation and form an ethical decision that seems the most loving, all things considered. The same act might be virtuous or evil, depending on the motive. The loving act might be to rob a bank, to kill someone, or to give away your shoes. All sorts of examples were concocted by these moralists, frequently in the area of human sexuality: Here is this poor woman who is unmarried and psychologically fouled up. What she really needs is a man. Now, if you sir, being a happily married man, really *love*, then you'll just do this young lady the self-sacrificing thing and have sexual relations with her. This will, no doubt, open up her personality and do her a great deal of good.

But how do you know that this girl might not end up far more unhappy and messed up than before because of your "loving" act? What about the guilt she may end up feeling? What of the sexually-transmitted disease she may pass on to you? What about the child that may be conceived? If you are going to fully compute the consequences you need to take into account what will happen in the life of the child and in society as a result of the birth. What if you conceive the next Joseph Stalin? How much good or love have you actually given?

Deeds

Some argue cogently that we cannot base ethical guidelines on the motive or the results of an action. That leaves us with the deed itself. This is a difficult path to take, without looking at motives or results. One popular approach is *statistical ethics*, determining morality by counting noses. How many believe it is right to kill people from Iowa? How many do not believe killing Iowans is a good idea? Only in a day of mass polling and demographic studies could such an ethic be possible. What is the proper sexual conduct for American families? Read *The Kinsey Report*! It tells what everybody's doing. Is abortion right or wrong? Consult the latest survey barometer of the standard. What is pornography? Most laws regarding pornography are established on the basis of statistical ethics: "prevailing community standards."

A rather obvious problem is that statistical ethics can only measure what *is*, never what *ought to be*. Kids have been using the statistical argument for years—

for millennia, probably ("But Dad, everybody's doing it!"). Few parents, certainly few intelligent parents, buy the statistical argument. You can never extract an *ought* from an *is*. Any decision can be justified through statistical data. All one must do is pick the public to sample. But what if we used a larger sample—the whole human race? But what if the entire human race is morally skewed? A universal sample could not be trusted, given the moral standards for the world.

The late Dr. Gordon Clark studied all possible ethical systems and stated unequivocally that no consistent ethical standard can be developed by the secular world. "It is their secularism," Clark said. "They are cut off from God." It is the cut-flower syndrome. The only health in secular ethics is that which has slipped in from Christianity. A cut-flower generation, without absolutes, is a sickly and degenerating way of life.

Connecting with the Source

Now that we have shot down most of the ethical systems around us, why do we think the Christian ethic meets the challenge? Why is our way superior?

First, the Christian ethic includes absolutes. It is wrong to murder someone in cold blood—always and under every circumstance. And we know the reason behind the absolute: Every human being is an image-bearer of God. Each life is in God's hand, and to take life is to take what belongs to God alone. We are not left in the dark about any of this. The rules are spelled out. We know how the game is played. In the case of murder, some of those instructions and warnings include Genesis 9:5–6; Exodus 20:13; Leviticus 24:17; Numbers 35:16–31; Proverbs 28:17; Revelation 21:8; 22:15. Further, Scripture deals with nations as well as individuals in assessing behavior (regarding the sanctity of life see, for example, Psalm 106:38; Isaiah 59:3–7; Jeremiah 7:9–10; Nahum 3:1; Matthew 23:35).

Second, Christian ethics have helpful parameters, which also are revealed to us. Is it murder to kill someone in war? What culpability does a person have if he kills to protect his or her own property or life? Are circumstances to be taken into account? What about accidental death? Is it murder when the state executes someone? Is an unborn child regarded as a person in relation to the laws regarding murder? Scripture covers each of these situations.

Third, Christian ethics alone of all ethical systems considers the thoughts as well as the actions of an individual (Ezekiel 35:5–6; Matthew 5:22; James 4:1–2; 1 John 2:9–11; 3:15).

Fourth, Christian ethics takes into account the larger motives behind the thoughts. In sanctity of life issues, for example, the motives God looks at include neglect or unconcern for others (Ezekiel 16:49; Matthew 25:31–46); passing judgment (Matthew 7:1–5; Romans 2:1–3; 14:2–4; James 4:12); feeling scorn (Proverbs 19:29; Isaiah 29:29; Jude 18), and slander (Matthew 15:19–20; Romans 1:30; Colossians 3:8; James 4:11).

Fifth, only Christian ethics of all ethical systems offers a twofold perfect standard by which to judge all thoughts, motives, and actions: *Love the Lord your God with all you are. Love your neighbor as yourself* (see Matthew 22:37–39).

Sixth, only Christian ethics offers redemption that transcends all actions and their penalties. If we murder we may have to suffer for our actions, but no mass murderer is beyond the reach of God's forgiveness.

Seventh, only Christian ethics has the indwelling power of the Holy Spirit in our hearts to work obedience and purity and holiness within us. Take away all other differences, and this alone gives ultimate freedom and joy to ethics. All other ethical systems are cut off from the Source. The Holy Spirit keeps us from being cut-flower people.

If we are going to live a successful Christian life, if we are going to be able to follow Jesus Christ and live according to the Christian ethic, it can only be done by the power of the Spirit of God. We say when we come to Jesus Christ that we will, by the power of his Holy Spirit endeavor to live lives as becomes the followers of Jesus Christ. But then we get into trouble because we forget. We endeavor to live lives that will glorify Jesus by our own strength and determination and will. This can never be. It is only the Spirit of God that gives us the power to live the Christian life. Ephesians 5:18 tells us: "Be not drunk with wine, wherein is excess; but, be filled with the Spirit." The Greek word for "be filled" means "to be continually getting filled" with the Spirit. The Holy Spirit comes to us through Jesus Christ. It is through Christ that we are enabled to have the Holy Spirit. God has given the Holy Spirit without measure to his Son. When we receive his Son we receive the Holy Spirit. But we are leaky vessels and need continually to be refilled with the power of God. This sets us apart from the cut-flower generation.

The *Westminster Confession* says that the Spirit of God subdues and enables our will, helping us freely and cheerfully to do the will of God that is revealed in the law. God's promise is not to give us a once-upon-a-time filling that leaves us struggling with our connectedness to God. It is not that the Holy Spirit leaves and we have to struggle to get more of him. He is fully inside every child of God, asking for more of us. God's promise for our life and living ethically is that, if we are thirsty for him, his Spirit will descend upon us abundantly:

I will pour water upon him that is thirsty, and floods upon the dry ground: I will pour my spirit upon thy seed, and my blessing upon thine offspring. [Isaiah 44:3]

God will give the Holy Spirit to those determined to obey him. It is only a lie of Satan that we can have just a little bit of fun through just a little bit of disobedience. At his right hand is joy forevermore, not at a distance from him, but just alongside. Why should we live as cut-flower people when connection is ours to enjoy, both now and forever?

What makes an ethical standard "Christian"?

Although true believers be not under the law as a covenant of works, to be thereby justified or condemned; yet is it of great use to them, as well as to others; in that, as a rule of life, informing them of the will of God and their duty, it directs and binds them to walk accordingly. [Westminster Confession of Faith, chapter 19]

2

Good Advice
and Good News

Scorching desert. Impenetrable clouds. Smoke as of a furnace. Leaping flames. Trembling mountain.

This was no movie set with special effects crew at work. Charlton Heston was not standing by in bearded makeup. It was one of the most significant moments in all history. The Creator of the universe had descended to give his creatures a reflection of his nature, a revelation of his will. He was establishing a set-apart way of life. In all other things God spoke through Moses or one of his prophets; now he came directly to the people. Their hearts melted, and they fell prostrate before thundering authority:

> I am the LORD thy God, which have brought thee out of the land of Egypt, out of the house of bondage. Thou shalt have no other gods before me.
>
> Thou shalt not make unto thee any graven image, or any likeness of any thing that is in heaven above, or that is in the earth beneath, or that is in the water under the earth: Thou shalt not bow down thyself to them, nor serve them. . . .

Thou shalt not take the name of the LORD thy God in vain [misuse it]; for the LORD will not hold him guiltless that taketh his name in vain.

Remember the sabbath day, to keep it holy. . . .

Honor thy father and thy mother. . . .

Thou shalt not kill.

Thou shalt not commit adultery.

Thou shalt not steal.

Thou shalt not bear false witness against thy neighbor.

Thou shalt not covet. . . .[Exodus 20:2–17]

The people drew back in terror and cried to Moses: "Speak thou with us, and we will hear: but let not God speak with us, lest we die" (20:19). Thus we received "ten words," ten commands of the moral law of God, from the voice of God.

Therefore we conclude that a man is justified by faith without the deeds of the law. . . . Do we then make void the law through faith? God forbid: yea, we establish the law. [Romans 3:28, 31]

Down through history individuals and nations have dashed themselves against that law, trying to break it. The fragments of their remains may be found in cemeteries, asylums, prisons, and skid rows. His law does not break; anyone who tries to break his law is broken.

Columnist Cal Thomas quoted a moralist who had addressed the National Press Club in Washington, D.C., with an ominous message about the state of America. This man warned: "At no time in my life has our culture been so estranged from spiritual values. . . . Our problems lie beyond the reach of politics alone." He went on to blame materialism and "a numbers-oriented culture based on what we can grasp and count. We have lost touch with the best of humanity—the inner life."

The speaker was Norman Lear—television producer and founder of People for the American Way. Lear has hardly distinguished himself as a friend of spiritual values. His philosophy has been part of the problem, instead of the solution. Lear and I do not agree on what needs to be done, yet we can agree on the diagnosis. Said Thomas of Lear's speech:

> Virtue, morals, respect for law and other people are not concepts that are caught like a strain of flu. They are not acquired by human nature. In fact, they must be taught, even imposed. . . . News reports suggest the beginning of what may be a spiritual revival in Russia. It appears many Russians are recovering what they once had but lost. It also appears too many Americans have abandoned what we once had but gave away— not to a dictator but to decadence. These two nations are like huge ships passing in the night, headed in opposite directions.

What Lear calls losing touch with the inner life, the Bible calls *lawlessness*. In 2 Thessalonians 2 Paul writes that the days before Christ returns will be an era of rebellion and lawlessness. Paul says of his own day that the power of lawlessness was already at work (2:7). Ours is an age where people have kicked off the traces and thrown off the restraints. On every side the moral law of God is abandoned. Within the church itself false teachers tell those who follow Jesus Christ: "You, too, may ignore the law of God. It does not apply to the believer, so live as you like."

Getting to know the law

It is good in these days of lawlessness to recognize that God's law still does apply—even to Christians. It applies *especially* to Christians.

"Oh, but we live under *grace* today!"

Yes, we do, so we must understand how the Bible keeps two great forces in tension—law and gospel. The law is important, for the unbeliever stands under its condemnation. But it helps the believer. As the *Westminster Confession of Faith* explains, Christians stand outside the *guilt* of the law; we are neither justified nor condemned by the thunder from the mountain. Yet, the Westminster framers remind us that the law still is a *rule for living*, especially for God's people. It is his good advice and far more: The law delineates principles of God's will for human behavior. To obey is nothing more than to act as an obedient child. Therefore, the law *directs* and, in a different sense than for the one outside of Christ, it *binds* the child of God.

Lots of laws are spread through the Old Testament. Are we to keep them all? We need to understand that God gave different types of laws for different purposes. Not all have the same importance today, but all have some meaning. People who say Christians are under none of the laws are called *antinomians* (*anti*, "against"; *nomos*, "law"). Another group teaches the opposite— that all laws (except sacrificial or temple laws) apply totally to all people and governments. These people are called *theonomists* and stir up serious arguments among those who want to take Scripture seriously but who do not want to apply Scriptures in ways God does not intend.

I suggest that we look to the laws for principles. What God hated he still hates; what he treated with approbation is still good. There are some judgment calls, some places requiring prayer, humility, and sanctified common sense. What follows attempts a simple overview of laws and what they mean today.

Foundation for a nation

When God brought the people of Israel out of Egypt his laws shaped a whining mob of ex-slaves into a nation—a uniquely set-apart people. This government was not to be ruled by King Moses or President Joshua. Leaders were God's intermediaries and the people's servants (a novel thought for politicians). Israel was not initially a monarchy or a democracy, but a *theocracy*—government by God. Therefore, although the laws were, in general, like other laws archeologists have discovered in ancient inscriptions, they also were distinctly different. *Civil, social, criminal, family,* and *ceremonial* laws in the Old Testament made this people radically God's. Jesus, in fact, made the meaning of the laws richer still, even as he took their penalties on himself. "Think not that I am come to destroy the law, or the prophets," he said in Matthew 5:17. "I am not come to destroy, but to fulfil."

So what do they mean if they are not *abolished* but *fulfilled* in Jesus' life and death? Jesus answered that all the commandments of God are summed up in two rules: (1) *Love God.* (2) *Love your neighbor.* Do such rules apply? Is not the church a people ruled by love? Said the Old Testament:

> Ye shall be unto me a kingdom of priests, and an holy nation. [Exodus 19:6a]

Wrote Peter to the church:

> But ye are a chosen generation, a royal priesthood, an holy nation, a peculiar people. [1 Peter 2:9a]

Adds John in Revelation 1:5b–6, we are to live in praise to Jesus—

> Unto him that loved us, and washed us from our sins in his own blood, and hath made us kings and priests unto God and his Father; to him be glory and dominion for ever and ever.

At Sinai the thunder from the mountain called for obedience to the God who had brought the people out of Egypt, out of the land of bondage. From the edge of the throne room in glory John calls us in Revelation 1 to obey the God who loves us and freed us out of sin, out of the land of bondage by his blood. The laws are organized as rules for civil interaction, criminal law, family life, social obligations, and religious life and worship.

Civil laws

Civil laws handle the private interaction and disputes between citizens, in which the state steps in as an arbiter. If a farmer borrows someone's ox and it dies, how should the disputing parties resolve the matter? If you borrow someone's Mazda and it dies. . . ? The Old

Testament offers basic principles of fairness and wisdom, good advice for a society that runs to the law courts at every turn. And for Christians the principle of fair play is tempered by the command to love. If I can show love to my neighbor in a dispute, even if it means worrying less about my own rights, God's love constrains my actions. Many non-Christians have been won to the Lord by seeing open-handed mercy when they expected tight-fisted self-interest. *The principle of God's civil law is that loving mercy extends the open hand to others.*

Criminal laws

Ancient Israel had a special covenant connection with God; therefore, we cannot apply their criminal laws in all aspects to our own government. Some laws seem harsh: Sabbath breaking, for example, was punishable by death, as was blasphemy. Man and woman offenders could be stoned to death for adultery. But in a theocracy, in which God was covenantally connected to the nation, any act that fundamentally violated the purity of the covenant relationship threatened national security. In the end Israel was destroyed because the people did not take seriously their obligation to remain undefiled.

And impurity is criminal in God's sight. We who are Christians also live in covenantal connection with God. Should we institute the death penalty for sinners in the church? This is hardly the prescription of the New Testament. Our personal relationship is founded in the blood of Christ and so is unbreakable. But not all who have their names on the church roll are God's people. We should love them and witness to them, but there are occasions for harsh sanctions, even excommunication from the church. Criminal immorality brings dishonor. I strongly believe that God punishes or has withdrawn from congregations—even denominations—who have not held themselves pure. Exercising church discipline must be done carefully, but the congregation that allows a practicing adulterer or a practicing malicious gossip to tear down the holiness of the body is in danger of a corporate death penalty (1 Corinthians 5:9–13; Revelation 2:5; 3:2–3, 16).

We also live under a civil government in which criminal acts given in God's law are rightly punished. As citizens we should promote an Old Testament principle that is often misunderstood. People say, "The Old Testament law was cruel, for it commanded us to take 'an eye for an eye and a tooth for a tooth.' How wonderful that Jesus canceled that law." Did he really? Here is what Jesus taught:

> Ye have heard that it hath been said, An eye for an eye, and a tooth for a tooth: But I say unto you, that ye resist not evil: but whosoever shall smite thee on thy right cheek, turn to him the other also. And whosoever shall compel thee to go a mile, go with him twain. Give to him that asketh thee, and from him that would borrow of thee, turn not thou away. [Matthew 5:38–39, 41–42]

Notice that Jesus does not say, "It is written." Rather, he remarks, "You have heard that it was said." Jesus is not dispatching Old Testament law into oblivion but correcting an invalid interpretation—that God allows private revenge. Quite the opposite is true. God's people are to prefer personal injustice against themselves to taking vengeance. Their attitude is to go beyond what people expect in forgiving. The criminal laws of the land do not come into the discussion at all, and Jesus never says that they no longer apply. Their principle is justice itself—Let the punishment fit the crime. Don't take barbaric delight in torturing the lawbreaker. And don't give preferential treatment to one evildoer over someone else who commits the same crime. God's criminal code took into account circumstances but never social standing. Judges were not to give preference in sentencing. Higher social status was not reason for easier punishment. Nor was punishment mitigated because of a difficult childhood or social disadvantage. "Let the punishment fit the crime," God demanded:

> So shalt thou put the evil away from among you. And those which remain shall hear, and fear, and shall henceforth commit no more any such evil among you. And thine eye shall not pity; but life shall go for life, eye for eye, tooth for tooth, hand for hand, foot for foot. [Deuteronomy 19:19b–21]

During its rare times of obedience Israel did inflict the death penalty and the lash, but their stress was on restitution of two, three, or four times the amount of damage, depending on the circumstances of the crime. Dehumanizing penal servitude was unknown. The principles of God's department of criminal justice were:

1. Purge the evil, by death or banishment if such extreme punishment is appropriate.
2. Make justice certain and painful enough that the law might be feared.
3. Use restitution and reconciliation of the offender when possible.
4. Fit the punishment to the crime.

We are not commanded to return our nation to Israel's theocracy, but we would do well to examine the principles of God's criminal law that apply to the household of faith and to society.

Family laws

In the ancient world most societies had similar family laws. Children were the property of parents, who held power of life and death. A wife was the property of the husband. She could own nothing. The husband was under a clan patriarch who had final say over the family circle. Israel was never more set apart than in its ideal for the family. Respect, obedience, and honor were demanded of children. Parents could not kill or treat their children cruelly. Marriage and divorce laws protected the woman to an extent unknown in other cultures. Women even could own property.

Some of these family laws sound strange in our culture, for they were tailored to the situations of that time. Still, the principles of the law apply today:

1. Husband, wife, and children owe mutual respect and honor.
2. A chain of loving, serving authority, with perfect equality, flows from God through husband to wife to children.
3. The family unit must be protected by the community in time of disaster.

Social laws

Some might say that we can still benefit from the principles of the civil, criminal, and family laws of the Old Testament, but they certainly lacked our cradle-to-grave social care. Yet look at the record: Our various plans for "warring on poverty" have come a long

way in cataloging all the ways that will *not* end
poverty. The more social programs at our disposal, the
more degrading poverty seems to become. Actually,
ancient Israel did not do so well in this arena either.
Greed and personal interests interfered with love, then
as now. But the Old Testament's humanitarian instructions covered a vast number of situations. Here are
some general principles:

1. Each person is responsible for helping those in
   need.
2. Financial and social status never affect an individual's worth.
3. The worshiping community provides the safety
   net.

The principle that each person helps his or her neighbor does not mean a handout, but a hand up. For example, loans must be repaid, but at no interest. If that
sounds impractical, I would point out that the average
interest rate for the ancient Near East was 25 percent
and up! Charging no interest was radical thinking in
that time, too. Is it better for government to dole out
money? The money runs out, but need keeps coming as
dependency dehumanizes generations of recipients.
Where Christians have taken Old Testament mandates
seriously, those in poverty have purchased homes
through creatively built and remodeled housing and
no-interest loans. They have learned to budget, parent, work, and keep surroundings clean, to pay for
what they receive or "glean" through food coopera-
tives and work programs. It is interesting how often
government praises the creative innovations of biblical social programs. But government seldom copies
their basic point—the respectful helping hand that
pulls those in poverty out of its degradation.

A last resort for a poor person who had fallen upon hard times in Israel was to sell himself into slavery. The law, however, forbade a Hebrew master from looking down on one who had become a servant, for God's law reminded that they had all been slaves in Egypt. The slave was to be provided for, treated with respect, and freed after no longer than seven years, with as much of a stake as the master could afford to break the cycle of poverty.

A return to slavery today is not the application; the principle is that love and respect offer a powerful force for change. A prison guard in Missouri was devastated to learn that his child had a life threatening illness requiring expensive treatment. As word got around about the family's plight one of the inmates figured there had to be some way to help. But how? Inmates could not have cash, and what little money they earned or their families sent to their accounts would do little. Undaunted, the inmate talked to believers who were part of the prison chapter of Jaycees. A plan evolved. A Jaycees photographer was allowed to take pictures to sell on family visiting days. Officers at the front desk handled the cash transactions. Hundreds of dollars accumulated toward the guard's medical bills. Other inmates became involved. For some it may have been the first time they had sought to help another without seeking something in return. Respecting love broke down barriers with creative love and the open hand. It testified that we all were once slaves in the land of bondage.

The worshiping community should provide for the helpless. God established no Department of Health and Human Services. Help flowed to the family from the worshiping community, not the government, when the breadwinner died, crops failed, or some other crisis knocked them off of their feet. Church and family partnership before God still provides the best safety net. How sad that we have turned over to government what is not a proper governmental task. We reap the results in high taxes, corruption, inefficiency, and programs that hurt more than help.

Religious laws

Ceremonial issues involved in the worship of God don't concern us today, do they? Let us look at the principles and see. God took a detailed interest in worship. Not just any form of worship would do. If an interesting form of ceremony was noticed among pagan idolaters, there was a simple rule to follow for using it to worship the true God: Don't!

We no longer go to a temple or have priests sacrifice animals to appease God's anger at our sins. But we still are part of that system. The Book of Hebrews tells us that the temple at Jerusalem has been superseded by the real temple of God's presence. A priest still intercedes for us—the Messiah Jesus. One sacrifice on the cross has replaced all the bulls and sheep and doves. They were a shadow of the real thing. When Christ, the substance, came, the shadows faded. No longer do we keep the Passover or the Day of Atonement, for Christ our Passover has accomplished it all (1 Corinthians 5:7).

Old Testament patterns do speak to us. First, God wants us to come before him in humility, repentance, praise, and thanksgiving. The form of worship must mirror the reality; worship must be in Spirit and in truth (John 4:24). Second, we are not to make up new ways to worship, though we have lots of room for creativity with those he has given. God's Word outlines worship. Third, time must be set aside for God. Though

Sunday as the day of resurrection has replaced the Saturday Sabbath, the Sabbath principle still works. It is good for us (see pp. 82–84). Those who must work on Sunday miss an important blessing and will be easily distracted from God if they do not find alternative times to come to him in worship and serving with a community of believers. Keeping a sabbath of service and worship can be difficult, but it seldom is impossible. Talk to your pastor about alternative ways to set aside time if your work schedule is a problem.

Law and gospel

Yes, we should study the Old Testament laws with joy, thankful that their precepts are good, even as their applications may have changed in the power of the gospel. All of the Bible basically contains two elements: law and gospel. We have looked at the fact that the gospel proclaims "good news." The Bible is not just "good advice"; neither is its basic message found in laws. The laws voiced from the mountain anticipated a night when angel voices burst the sky: "We bring you glad tidings of good news." The good news is that those who have not followed the good advice from the mountain can have God's mercy. Only after trusting in Christ for the good news of God's grace—only after being redeemed from the penalty for lawbreaking—do we find that the commandments of God show a lifestyle that pleases God and that works.

But like everything else in the spiritual sphere, we confuse good advice with good news. Suppose you live in rural America of a century ago. One day you go to the city. To your amazement you discover that horses are not being used to pull carts. Instead, people have rigged their buggies so the horses push the carts. Confusion reigns. People sit in their buggies, staring eyeball to eyeball at their horses, pleading with them to "Giddyap! Push! Push!" Somehow it doesn't work nearly as well. You can only shake your head at the incredible stupidity of these city folks.

But look around at a society that once had a Christian superstructure and churches where the gospel was declared. Everyone from Norman Lear on down looks for a moral structure without the gospel. Although they may not admit it, they want some version of God's good advice because deep inside they know that some things are right and some are wrong. Yet, in their godless versions of God's good advice they refuse to recognize absolutes. They have hooked up the buggy backwards and substituted the horse with a blind laboratory rat. At this writing Russia has enormous problems to overcome after three-quarters of a century under communism. But Thomas is right in his column: Millions of the Russian people are "rushing toward God like a repentant sinner," while the West runs toward self-salvation. New laws go on the books each year, but no good news.

Every other religion in the world, except atheism and paganism, speaks from law. The law says: "Keep me in order to have merit before God. Do this. Do that. Don't do something else." Christianity sets the horse before the cart. Christ says, "I am the Lord, your God, who can bring you out of the land of death through my blood, out of the house of bondage to sin. I change your heart and give you salvation and my Spirit. *Therefore*, keep my commands. Having first been brought to God, we do these things. The difference between Christianity and the other religions of the world is the difference between *in order to* and *therefore*.

"The world has many religions," said George Owen. "It has but one gospel." When people say, "All religions are the same," they are saying that Christianity, like the others, is all *do* and *don't do*. It is an *in order to* sort of faith. In other world religions men and women must reach up and somehow find God. The word *religion* means "bind oneself to." Only in Christianity is God reaching down to men and women. Only the real God does what is necessary for us to be reconciled to him. The basic message of Christianity is not *do* but *done*. "It is finished!" were Christ's words on the cross (John 19:30). It is complete! It is enough! The gospel is not a challenge to do; it is an offer to receive.

What the law does

What, then, does the law do for those who are outside of Christ? First, it reveals their sin. Second, it reveals how bad our sin truly is. Third, it actually makes people more rebellious and sinful. Fourth, it shows how hopeless the situation is.

The law reveals sin

Without understanding sin, no one would understand the need for Christ. "I had not known sin, but by the law," explains Paul. "I had not known lust, except the law had said, Thou shalt not covet." (Romans 7:7; see also Romans 2:15). Many do not realize that lusting in the heart is adultery in the sight of God, or that anger in the heart is murder in the sight of God. When the law reveals these things, we see our guilt.

The law reveals the awfulness of sin

The law shows us how guilty guilt is. People want to live in the grays. They don't want to be "evil," really. They want just to sample the edges of evil, to push the boundaries a bit. God's ethics knows no middle ground. There are no "white" lies. Lies are black and abominable to a God who is total truth. His eyes are too pure to look upon shades of sin. All sin means corruption, and he cannot but punish it.

The law aggravates the motions of sin

You are driving down the street at fifty miles an hour. The radio plays a song you like, and all is well with the world. Suddenly you pass a sign that declares: "Speed limit 25." The law has come and declares that you are not in conformity. Now there is struggle. Will you continue to sail along at fifty or reduce your speed? You don't want to reduce your speed. You are in a hurry. You are late for an appointment. You feel rebellious that fences are set around choices. Law makes sin into struggle.

John Bunyan in *The Pilgrim's Progress* explains this nicely. The hero of his story, "Pilgrim," is taken into a large, beautifully appointed parlor. However, it has not been dusted or swept in many a year. Cobwebs are thick. His companion, "Interpreter," calls in a maiden with a broom and bids her to sweep. The dust she stirs up chokes Christian until he asks its meaning. Interpreter replies, "This is the work of the law in the heart. The dust is the sin that is accumulated there for years, and then the law comes and stirs it up."

Romans 5:20 says that "law entered, that the offence might abound." It stirs up sin that we choke on it. In the story, Interpreter calls in another maiden and bids her sprinkle the room with water. Once the dust settles it is easily cleansed. These, he explains, are the sweet influences of the dew of the gospel, which takes away and makes easily removable the sin in our hearts.

The law shows human hopelessness

How well must one keep the law to be accepted? By now you should immediately hear the answer: "Perfectly." A number of years ago my wife and I had dinner at the home of one of our church families. Seated across from me was the hostess's mother, a woman of about seventy. She said to me, "Oh, Reverend Kennedy, I am so happy to be able to ask you something I've always wanted to ask a minister. How good does a person have to be to be good enough to get into heaven?"

"Oh, that is an easy question to answer."

Her face broke into a huge smile. "Do you mean you *know*? You'll never know how relieved I am. I have been worrying about that for years."

"You'll never need to worry about the answer to that question again. Jesus said it very clearly: 'Be perfect, as your heavenly Father is perfect'" [see Matthew 5:48].

She looked like a cartoon character that had been hit by a skillet! She sat silently for a long time, then said, "I think I'm going to worry about that more than ever."

"I did not go into the ministry to make people worry, but to deliver them from their worries," I assured her. Then I shared the gospel of Jesus Christ: Though none of us lives up to God's standard, Jesus came to do what we have been unable to do. The law shows how much we need Christ.

For as many as are of the works of the law are under the curse: for it is written, Cursed is every one that continueth not in all things which are written in the book of the law to do them. But that no man is justified by the law in the sight of God, it is evident: for, The just shall live by faith. And the law is not of faith: but, The man that doeth them shall live in them. Christ hath redeemed us from the curse of the law, being made a curse for us: for it is written, Cursed is every one that hangeth on a tree: That the blessing of Abraham might come on the Gentiles through Jesus Christ; that we might receive the promise of the Spirit through faith. [Galatians 3:10–14]

The great difference

What then is the difference between law and gospel?

The law binds the unbeliever; the gospel of grace frees the believer to obey God's will.

The law is condemnation; the gospel of grace is mercy and justification.

The law convicts; the gospel of grace relieves.

The law produces rebellion; the gospel of grace produces submission.

The law depresses us with inability; the gospel of grace delivers us in power.

The law produces pride in those who suppose they can make the passing grade; the gospel of grace produces thankfulness in those who know they cannot, those who have been accepted anyway.

The law says, "Do in order to"; the gospel of grace says, "Done."

The law says, "Go and work"; the gospel of grace says, "Come to Christ for rest."

We are not saved by the law; we are not saved by the gospel plus the law; we are not saved by faith plus works. We are saved by faith alone, forgiven, and empowered to keep the law in its purest form of love.

How is life made free in Christ?

he liberty which Christ hath purchased for believers under the gospel consists in their freedom from the guilt of sin, the condemning wrath of God, the curse of the moral law; and in their being delivered from this present evil world, bondage to Satan, and dominion of sin, from the evil of afflictions, the sting of death, the victory of the grave, and everlasting damnation.
[Westminster Confession of Faith, chapter 20]

3

"Give Me Liberty!"

We in the West face a subtle adversary in humanism, the philosophy that humankind is the measure of all things, and that spiritual values are irrelevant, or dangerous. The subtlety and seriousness of the enemy was forced into my consciousness as I spoke with someone and happened to mention Patrick Henry.

"Who?" she asked.

It turned out this was not a momentary memory lapse. This young woman, as best she could recall, had honestly never heard of the Christian statesman and orator who, perhaps more than any other, ignited the sparks that caused the independence of this nation to come to pass. Then I remembered reading that some history texts have expunged the name of Henry and the speech for which he is most famous, his call to "Give me liberty or give me death!" Henry's thundering sentiment, I understand, is not deemed appropriate to teach. It is thought inconsistent with the ideal of peaceful coexistence and acceptance of others. Back in the anti-war protest days this feeling was summed up in that heart-fluttering cry from the college campus: "Better red than dead!"

Henry was hardly a menace to world order. In fact, he was elected governor of Virginia six times. Yet on

the day he made the statement he was only a specta-
tor in the Virginia House of Burgesses. He listened with
growing frustration as the delegates considered why
the colonies should not
go too far in offending
mother England. When
he could stomach no
more of it he rose to his
feet, at first speaking
softly, then building up
a crescendo of passion:

> *Now the Lord is that Spirit: and where the Spirit of the Lord is, there is liberty.*
> [2 Corinthians 3:17]

They tell us, sir, that
we are weak—unable
to cope with so for-
midable an adver-
sary. But when shall
we be stronger? Will
it be the next week,
or the next year?
Will it be when we
are totally disarmed, and when a British guard shall
be stationed in every house? Shall we gather strength
by irresolution and inaction? Shall we acquire the
means of effectual resistance by lying supinely on our
backs, and, hugging the delusive phantom of hope, until
our enemies shall have bound us hand and foot?

As he continued his words became thunderbolts
falling on the seats around him. People moved forward
in their seats and strained their necks to see who was
talking. He concluded:

There is a just God who presides over the destinies of
nations, and who will raise up friends to fight our bat-
tles for us. The battle, sir, is not to the strong alone; it
is to the vigilant, the active, the brave. Besides, sir, we

have no election. If we were base enough to desire it, it is now too late to retire from the contest. There is no retreat but in submission and slavery. Our chains are forged. Their clanking may be heard on the plains of Boston. The war is inevitable, and let it come! I repeat it, sir: Let it come!

It is in vain, sir, to extenuate the matter. Gentlemen may cry peace, peace—but there is no peace. The war is actually begun! The next gale that sweeps from the north will bring to our ears the clash of resounding arms! Our brethren are already in the field! Why stand we idle here? What is it that gentlemen wish? What would they have? Is life so dear, or peace so sweet, as to be purchased at the price of chains and slavery?

Forbid it, Almighty God! I know not what course others may take, but as for me, give me liberty or give me death!

As he finished, such astonishment fell upon the legislators that most could think of only one course of action. They took steps that would lead inexorably toward revolution and American independence.

The meaning of liberty

When Christians speak of liberty they often narrow the focus to questions of how freely we may behave and still be considered saved. People want to know what they can get by with. Some of this discussion has been practical and important in dealing with matters that are not specifically addressed in the Bible. An example is whether Christians should participate in the secular trappings of Christmas and Easter, decorating trees, giving presents, and hiding colored eggs. Other examples involve what kinds of songs may be sung in worship or whether Christians have liberty of conscience about whether to run for public office, drink alcoholic beverages, dance, play cards, go to movies, own a television, smoke, participate on a jury, carry a gun in the military, work in a store that sells *Playboy,* or a large variety of other matters. Each issue involves its own underlying biblical principles, even if the activity itself is not specifically mentioned in Scripture.

But a larger question of liberty must be answered before we counsel or condemn. If we seem to regulate behavior without laying the groundwork of understanding what Christian liberty means, we surely will come off as the self-righteous prigs many in the secular world believe Christians to be.

Any biblical discussion of Christian liberty proceeds from the attitude of a Patrick Henry, an attitude of controlled, disciplined defiance in the face of force. A few of his listeners must have thought Patrick was making a lot of fuss. "Aw, come on! We don't have it so bad. The English tax our tea, and their laws are rather arbitrary, but after all, we are just a weak little colony. Why rock the boat?"

"NO!" was the rejoinder. "A greater principle is involved than taxes, and some principles are more important than life itself. Giving them up voluntarily is not an option." Henry was not concerned that life would be more carefree if Americans didn't have to pay taxes for tea. The control of the national destiny of America was the issue. Here was a non-negotiable.

Now listen to another voice that began to speak softly but soon was roaring with indignant passion:

> I marvel that ye are so soon removed [literally, becoming a turncoat] from him that called you into the grace of Christ unto another gospel: Which is not another; but there be some that trouble you, and would pervert the gospel of Christ. But though we, or an angel from

heaven, preach any other gospel unto you than that which we have preached unto you, let him be accursed. As we said before, so say I now again, if any man preach any other gospel unto you than that ye have received, let him be accursed. [Galatians 1:6–9]

Surely some people in the Galatian church were surprised by the hot words. "Cool down, Paul. Aren't you getting exercised over very little? What can it hurt if we set a few stipulations on people coming into the church? We still look to God for our salvation. We only want to add something. People will be saved by grace, *and. . . .* "

"NO!" came the rejoinder. "A greater principle is involved—the very freedom for which the Son of God died, the freedom of grace over sin and death. That freedom is no option. If anyone tries to throw away the atonement of Christ, let him be damned!"

That was the attitude with which the framers of the *Westminster Confession of Faith* gathered in the midst of the English Civil War to set forth principles they believed were worth dying for. These men knew that, should their king be victorious over the forces of Parliament in this bloody war, all of their lives might well be forfeit.

When they came to their own statement, "Of Christian Liberty, and Liberty of Conscience," they wrote carefully and sought balance. "God alone is Lord of the conscience," they declared, "and hath left it free from the doctrines and commandments of men which are in any thing contrary to his Word, or beside it in matters of faith or worship." All people did not have to believe as they did. However, no human government or doctrine or church had the right to bind the destiny of God's people to a philosophy that violated God's

Word. Liberties purchased by the blood of Christ were non-negotiable:

> Christ purchased freedom from the guilt of sin.
> Christ purchased freedom from the condemning wrath of God.
> Christ purchased freedom from the curse of the law.
> Christ purchased freedom from bondage to an evil world system.
> Christ purchased freedom from bondage to Satan.
> Christ purchased freedom from the dominion of sin.
> Christ purchased freedom from the afflictions brought on the body by sin.
> Christ purchased freedom from the power of death, the grave, and everlasting damnation.

The *Confession* makes a connection that American Christians seem to have forgotten, though it has been proven by world history. The moral ethic of civil liberty and the Christian reality of spiritual liberty interlocked. Where Christianity has become a vital force in society, freedom and liberty have expanded. Does this equate loving America with loving God? Some have mistakenly made that connection and created an idolatrous civil religion. However, the principles that built stable, freedom-living democracies in the Christian West have grown out of the hearts of those who love God. Christians who understood biblical freedom in Christ were salty enough that they influenced the creation of an American Constitution. Even those who hated Christianity among the framers of the Constitution were profoundly aware that its ethical principles worked. They knew that where men's and women's hearts were truly different in the liberty of Christianity, their behavior was more caring and serving. Where the Spirit of the Lord was, there was liberty.

That first became obvious one day in an ancient synagogue in Nazareth when a young local man who was making a name for himself as a rabbi stood and unrolled the scroll of the prophet Isaiah (61:1–2a). He read:

> The spirit of the Lord GOD is upon me; because the LORD hath anointed me to preach good tidings unto the meek; he hath sent me to bind up the broken-hearted, to proclaim liberty to the captives, and the opening of the prison to them that are bound; to proclaim the acceptable year of the LORD.

Jesus announced in that moment that he came to proclaim deliverance—to set the captives free. We know that the great work of Christ is the work of redemption, to "buy back out of bondage," to restore from slavery. "Stand fast therefore in the liberty wherewith Christ hath made us free" Paul said (Galatians 5:1). Jesus said, "If the Son therefore shall make you free, ye shall be free indeed" (John 8:36). Right away two implications of the freedoms listed in the *Westminster Confession* become obvious: First, this list in no way invites us to "get by" with loose living. We are freed from the bondage of sin to live in Christ's presence. Our conscience is unchained from the guilt of a lifetime in sin without Christ. We are unchained from rebellion against God. Paul advises us that, since we were called to be free, "use not liberty for an occasion to the flesh, but by love serve one another" (Galatians 5:13). This is an invitation to self-discipline. Second, this freedom is that of a freed slave, so it certainly doesn't make Christians better than anyone else. Among Christians "there is neither Jew nor Greek, there is neither bond nor free, there is neither male nor female: for ye are all one in Christ Jesus" (Galatians 3:28). Among other unbelievers we are called to continue the task of proclaiming liberty to the captives. Now, imagine what that attitude does to the life of a nation founded upon Christian principles. To the extent those principles are known and believed, exactly to that extent government establishes true freedom and justice for all. Where humanistic principles are believed and proclaimed there is no reason not to cheat and enslave, for there is no absolute standard for justice (see pp. 23–32).

The loss of liberty

The American Declaration of Independence and Constitution were written, we are told, to secure, among other things, the blessings of liberty to ourselves and our children. Throughout the long history of this world, those times and places where people have enjoyed true liberty have been few. The vast majority of people have never enjoyed the blessings of liberty. These blessings, so rare, are easily taken for granted. Liberty cannot be seen, tasted, or smelled. Those who have it come to prize it not at all. In the late 1980s and early 1990s, a group of nations began to feel the new birth of freedom after decades under a totalitarian rule. Yet we saw how fragile, indeed, that freedom could be in the civil wars and political unrest that followed. George Orwell was a journalist who saw firsthand the influences of Nazism and communism. Then, to his horror, he saw his own England being subverted by a strong communist movement during World War II. His warning to England was the bitter allegorical story *Animal Farm*—a description of what was at risk. He was asked one time about his vision of the future. "The future," he said, "is a picture of a boot stomping on the face of a man forever." Without faith in the Christ who

proclaimed liberty to the captives, Orwell could see no
hope for liberty. And without the Christ who proclaims
liberty, Orwell is correct.

Abraham Lincoln, who was a Christian, understood
better the danger and the hope: "Our fathers brought
forth upon this continent a new nation, conceived in
liberty. . . . Now we are engaged in a great civil war,
testing whether that nation, or any nation so conceived
and so dedicated, can long endure."

I am afraid modern blessings of liberty are threatened in some of the same ways the government of
Charles II threatened the freedoms of English citizens
in the era before the Westminster Assembly. Not all Bill
of Rights liberties are made sacred by Scripture, and
the writers of the *Confession* said Christian liberty is
not a pretense to "oppose any lawful power, or the lawful exercise of it, whether it be civil or ecclesiastical."
Yet there is a place to stand with Patrick Henry in defiance of societies or governments or the powers of
demons. No legitimate power on earth or in heaven or
hell can impinge upon that liberty that, "being delivered out of the hands of our enemies, we might serve
the Lord without fear, in holiness and righteousness
before him, all the days of our life." Does this statement from the *Confession* chapter 20 repeat a familiar
strain?

"What is our chief purpose for existing?" asked the
Westminster writers.

"To glorify God and enjoy him forever," came their
answer.

Who has given us the freedom to fulfil God's ultimate purpose for us?

God in Christ has died and risen so that we might
freely glorify and enjoy him.

Who dare trade that freedom for fake self-
righteousness on one side or unholy living that makes

light of Christ's death on the other? Even if angels teach such things, let them be damned.

"Is life so dear, or peace so sweet, as to be purchased at the price of chains and slavery? Forbid it, Almighty God! I know not what course others may take, but as for me, give me liberty or give me death!"

I am afraid that our blessings of liberty are under great threat for want of men and women whose love extends to sacrifice. Spiritual liberty, and even liberty to live as a disciplined citizen, come out of hearts that know liberty in Jesus Christ, for where the Spirit of the Lord is, there is liberty. Martin Luther used to refer to himself as *Martin Elutheras. Elutheras* is the Greek word for "free." In Christ he was *Martin the Free.* Does the name *Elutheras* belong to you as well? Have you been set free by Jesus Christ? If Christ has set you free, the Spirit of God dwells in your heart and there is a burning flame for Christian liberty. I am confident that all of the oppressors and all of the tyrants in all of the world will not be able to finally stamp out that flame. We need men and women with that burning passion for Christ and for the freedom that he alone can give—a freedom from sin and a freedom from tyranny and oppression.

For want of such men and women the Christian witness in America has withdrawn over the last century. The church stopped moving forward to proclaim liberty in every sphere of life. A defective view of Christianity, called *pietism*, produced this retreat. Pietism emphasized a very personal and private spirituality. Personal spirituality is good. But pietism excludes the world. Instead of effecting positive change, pietists confine spirituality to their own lives. The very first mandate God gave us in the Garden of Eden is ignored, to subdue the earth and have dominion over it (Genesis 1:28). God called his creatures to involvement in the business of the world. That mandate was never rescinded by the fall into sin, though it became a great challenge in a world degraded by sin and shame. As pietism pushed the faithful into their holy corner, ominous movements crept in and various spheres were turned over to the unbelievers. The movements slowly became crowding weeds in the garden of liberty, imperiling religious freedoms in the arts, the media, science, law, politics, the social sciences, and education. The authority and genius behind these movements is satanic. Their intent is to take away, where possible, the authority and ability to glorify God and enjoy him in the very spheres of life most important to subduing and ruling creation today.

Our adversaries have willingly persevered and watched for each step back. Paul Blanshard, one of the best known humanist educators in America, wrote an article in *Humanist* magazine looking back over the last seventy-five years. He noted with satisfaction that those years were "full of rebellion against religious superstition." In fact, he also says that after sixteen years in school Johnny may not be able to read, but at least we have rid his mind of the religious superstition that he brought to school from home. Blanshard goes on to say that he doubts that any span in human history has carried the world farther along to honest doubt. Robert C. Hawley, an architect of values clarification education, wrote in his book *Human Values in the Classroom* that the battle for humanistic values is not yet won:

> Still, we must make a beginning. And we can see already signs of hope in such things as the increasing interest in the open classroom, individualized instruction, integrated-day-type classrooms, schools-without-walls, alternative schools, etc. But these beginnings

have still left the lives of millions and millions of children unchanged. We must persist, we must step up our efforts, we must persevere: The time is growing short, the time to teach the human values is now, the time to teach survival is at hand.

Anyone who has followed the course of education since 1973 when this book was published knows that some of the great steps Dr. Hawley foresaw have been tried and have failed and been dropped by educators. But those ideas were not the real agenda. They only were signs of moving in the right direction. The goal was to "teach human values," to replace the old educational measures of excellence and absolutes with a moral philosophy of relativism and human-centered religion. And the fruits of those advances have devastated a generation. John J. Dunphy wrote, also in *Humanist*,

I am convinced that the battle for human kind's future must be waged and won in the public school classroom by teachers who correctly perceive their role as proselytizers of a new faith. . . . They will be ministers of another sort, utilizing a classroom instead of a pulpit to convey humanist values in whatever subject they teach. The classroom must and will become an arena of conflict between the old and the new—the rotting corpse of Christianity . . . and the new faith of humanism.

These visionaries have pushed on toward their goal—what they saw as a better world. Their vision is stronger and clearer than that of many Christians. Such atheistic leaders believed in the importance of fighting for their mission persistently and patiently. True, its end has already achieved the destruction of important aspects of liberty, but the humanists seek what they see as a greater ideal—an ideal they view as non-negotiable.

Their ideal has advanced for want of more Patrick Henrys in the church. We left the field, and our more dedicated opponents were waiting. The same has happened in every sphere of life, even the church.

One of the most disastrous consequences has involved the law, as judges reinterpreted the First Amendment to push Christians aside. The founding fathers of America believed something diametrically opposed to what is taught now about the First Amendment. Does the First Amendment teach the separation of church and state? Ask almost any person on the street today and that person will say that, of course, it does. Everybody knows that. Separation has become the overwhelming assumption and a legal doctrine is justified by this interpretation. Yet any objective study of the Bill of Rights and the background of the First Amendment shows that this is not so. The founding fathers of this country resolved the issue of church and state in a marvelously balanced fashion. The First Amendment states:

> Congress shall make no law respecting an establishment of religion or forbidding the free exercise thereof.

What does that say about what the church can and cannot do? What does that say about what the citizen should or should not do? It says nothing about such things. It says nothing about the church whatever. The rule does not protect the state from the church; it protects the church from the state.

Where, then, did we get this idea of a "wall of separation between church and state"? It comes from a letter Thomas Jefferson angrily wrote in 1802 to Baptists and Congregationalists in Danbury, Connecticut, because they had attacked him when he ran for President. They had called him an infidel, an atheist, and a few other uncomplimentary things. In his letter he told them, in effect, to shut up and stay in their place. He said there should be "a wall of separation between church and state." Jefferson certainly was welcome to his opinion, and certainly he was not the only one who has felt that way. That is not, however, what went into the Constitution, and it is my opinion that Jefferson himself would not have wanted to put it there once he got over his snit with the Baptists. Not all the framers of the Constitution were Christians. Not all were deists either, as some historians seem to believe. Whatever their religion, however, they valued a stable government and found the most tested and successful values for that stability in the Bible. What they did not appreciate was the custom of government supporting one religion with tax dollars or passing laws mandating presence in Sunday services.

The criminality of Christ

Our religious liberties as Americans depend on understanding the difference between protecting religion from the state and protecting the state from religion. The First Amendment is a one-way street. All of the Bill of Rights—the first ten amendments to the Constitution—was written to restrain the federal government from interfering with the liberties of the people. Their very reason for the passage of the Bill of Rights amendments to the Constitution was that those at the constitutional convention were afraid of a centralized government and refused to accept one unless the rights of the people were further defined and protected.

And their very first right priority guaranteed freedom of religion and expression, both of which are regularly denied to Christians. The wall of separation doctrine that made a private letter into public constitutional law is emphatically a two-way street. It prohibits and restrains both state and church. But even that two-way protection has been denied by some major church-state decisions of the last thirty years. Courts have tended to restrict the church and allow as little interaction from the church side as possible. That is exactly 180 degrees from what those at the constitutional convention—I suspect even Jefferson—would have wanted.

Several years ago the state of California moved to tackle one of its great criminal activities—home Bible studies. The newspaper account of this action said that the Bible studies were shut down despite the fact that the people said they would not sing songs and would disperse their cars. They were told that if one person outside the family was involved in studying the Bible it was an unlawful church activity. How far is this from the long-standing persecution of unofficial house churches in China? Actually it is even more restrictive, for these Bible studies were not even acting as churches, as do the illegal Chinese bodies.

California also made headlines some years back with a survey that went out to the churches asking such questions as: "Have you in the past year made any statements concerning such political matters as abortion? homosexual rights? ERA?" More than eighty churches declined to answer such statements, and their churches were immediately thrown onto the tax rolls. Buildings were confiscated. Such an outcry went up that the intolerable tyranny was stopped, but this is the kind of action and reaction taking place. The government most recently has moved to apply antiracketeering charges against abortion protesters. We may soon see a test case in which an organized church that speaks out against the murder of unborn children will be charged with being an organized crime ring.

Another ominous tendency is seen in the legal revolution going on in the West. Ask the person on the street the question: "Can you legislate morality?" The answer will come back: "Of course you can't, and you shouldn't try." If you can't legislate morality, what can you legislate? Immorality? The fact is that you cannot legislate anything but morality. We have laws against stealing because it is immoral to steal; rape because it is immoral to rape. The issue is whose morality is being legislated. Recent attempts to legislate home schools out of existence—even when the home schooled children do exceptionally well in achievement tests—operate from the premise that the only moral way to educate children is in schools. Society has an obligation to protect children from the immoral educational standards imposed by the home schooling parents. Refusing to hire an active homosexual has been declared immoral in the halls of legislatures and courts. Increasingly Western conceptions of immorality are quite clearly those actions or beliefs that do not conform to the humanist agenda. Look closely at any law or court decision that seems wrong-headed or controverted in its reasoning. Someplace under the surface something is being declared moral and something else immoral. Usually it isn't too hard to figure whose morality is being legislated.

The American legislative system was founded upon the Judeo-Christian ethic of the founding fathers. Jefferson wrote the charter for the University of Virginia that the proofs for God as the sovereign Lord and Creator and Ruler of this world and of the moral requirements and obligations that flow from that, must be taught to all students. Is this the same wall-of-separation Jefferson? One would almost think he approved of a theistic ethic at the very foundation of education's contributions to society and government. Perhaps he didn't mind religion's place in moral leadership; he simply disliked Baptist preachers who got personal about it.

Significant changes have appeared in the moral fabric of legislative and judicial theory. One worldview system seeks to push away another. Once the substitution is complete society may be very alien in its approach to human rights and freedoms than anything known to date. Think of the changes that have appeared in the last half century in the areas of infanticide, euthanasia, homosexuality, marriage and divorce, pornography, gambling, suicide. . . . This is not to say that the founding fathers were moral giants or that our grandparents of fifty years ago did not see fundamental flaws in the character of their society and government. All governments, from the national to the local levels, have blind spots, and ours have been serious. Liberty and equality for all has been more of an ideal than a reality. But it was an ideal even when it wasn't practiced or applied justly. A moral ethic operated, even when people didn't cooperate with it. James Madison, the primary author of the U.S. Constitution, said that we cannot govern without God and the Ten Commandments. The Supreme Court Building in Washington, D.C., has those Ten Commandments inscribed on its wall. Yet the Ten Commandments cannot be put up on the walls of a school in Kentucky. Why? The Supreme Court says doing so violates the Constitution that Madison wrote.

The call to non-negotiables

The wise and godly Bible teacher John Murray said that it is impossible to segregate ethics from the transcendent holiness, righteousness, and truth of God taught in Scripture. We may draw from this a linked chain of truths:

Only when the church holds a high view of a holy God and his self-revealing, inerrant Word to be non-negotiable does it have the moral ability to understand Christian liberty and its limits.

Only when an individual Christian submits himself or herself to a holy God through believing in Jesus Christ and repenting of sins is Christian liberty in its fullest sense possible.

Only when the individual Christian becomes mature in sanctification will some questions about Christian liberty fall into place. Meanwhile, be careful not to offend God or a weaker brother or sister by pushing to the limits of ethical propriety. Yet imposing ethical restrictions on oneself or others without strong biblical warrant also offends God and fellow Christians (see, for example, Romans 14 and 1 Corinthians 8).

Only when individual Christians join Christ in proclaiming liberty and living in it will they become salt and light in local and national public life.

Only when secular governments honor and listen to the Judeo-Christian faith of Scripture will liberty become important enough to be a non-negotiable once again.

How is life made rich in Christ?

*A*s it is of the law of nature, that, in general, a due proportion of time be set aside for the worship of God; so in his Word, by a positive, moral, and perpetual commandment, binding all men in all ages, he hath particularly appointed one day in seven for a Sabbath, to be kept holy unto him; which, from the beginning of the world to the resurrection of Christ, was the last day of the week; and, from the resurrection of Christ, was changed into the first day of the week, which in Scripture is called the Lord's day, and is to be continued to the end of the world, as the Christian Sabbath. [Westminster Confession of Faith, chapter 21]

4

A Day Saved for Eternity

*I*n the last chapter I considered that God has given us the liberty to fulfil our chief reason for existing—to glorify and enjoy him forever. We looked at some of the ways our enemy seeks to rob us of that liberty in Christ and how seriously the apostle Paul viewed any attempt to steal away what Christ has given to us. He angrily called down God's damnation upon human or angel who would subvert what belongs to the believer by heritage.

I wonder, though, should Paul walk around our nation on a typical Sunday, if he might not first vent his anger upon those who do not bother using what they possess. Do most Christians really want to enjoy God's company and fellowship? Do they wish to truly enjoy him through eternity? Do not our Sundays tell a different story? In the mid-1980s one of the last large cities to keep at least a token set of restrictions on Sabbathday commerce was St. Louis County in Missouri. Time and society had eroded away most of the laws' enforcement, but some groups were miffed that government might still abide by the archaic custom of "blue laws." Particularly harmful was the fact that package liquor stores and most bars and restaurants were not allowed to serve alcohol on Sundays. A referendum was put on the ballot, and it received a lot of publicity. Some Christians campaigned fervently under the banner of the S.O.S. (Save Our Sunday) organization. They waged an heroic battle, but few were surprised that the election resoundingly voted to strip the legal codes of their Sunday provisions. Evidently not many who would have identified themselves as Christians cared to set aside a special day for worship and rest. Why should they? Some of them had stopped even attending church, and though many did go, at least occasionally, the day had become nothing truly special. It was a time for enjoying time off work to sleep in, golf, watch sports programs, or be with the family. Monday would do as well. Is Sunday anything special to God? Didn't the Sabbath used to be on Saturday anyway?

> *Remember the Sabbath Day, to keep it holy. Six days shalt thou labor and do all thy work, but the seventh day is the sabbath to the LORD thy God.* [Exodus 20:8–10]

Remember the Sabbath

When Adam walked out of Eden he took with him two institutions that have immeasurably blessed the human race—the institution of the home, and one even older, the Sabbath. The Sabbath was the first institution God gave. Its benefit can hardly be overestimated. An old maxim states: "As goes the Sabbath, so goes the nation." We might do well to ponder that thought in the light of what happened in St. Louis, which was one of the last holdouts of a set-aside Sabbath. We live in a time when the Sabbath has come under great attack from several different points of view. There are those who declare that Christ abolished it, so it no longer is in effect. That view badly distorts what Christ said, that he is Lord of the Sabbath (Matthew 12:8; see Matthew 12:1–13). Jesus abolished some teachings that were circulating in his day about the Sabbath. It is right, above all else, to do acts of love and mercy on that day. It is not designed to be a burden but a blessing. One may certainly take care of what needs to be done. But abolish the Sabbath? If he is Lord of it, he surely plans to keep it around. The Scriptures at no point teach that Christ annulled, abrogated, or abolished any of the Ten Commandments. On the contrary, the Scriptures plainly teach that the Commandments remain in effect and have been strengthened by Christ, who declared that we are to keep them in thought, word, and deed if we love him (see pp. 42–43).

It is interesting that when Jesus describes the end of the world, his second coming, and the destruction of Jerusalem in A.D. 70 (Matthew 24), he tells his followers to pray that their flight from the great calamity befalling the nation will not be in the winter nor on the Sabbath (v. 20). Bible scholars divide over whether Jesus refers here to an event at the end of the world, or to the destruction of Jerusalem forty years later. If it was the latter he meant the time when the New Testament was mostly written and the New Testament church well established. He certainly intended that the Sabbath would continue.

But did he intend that Sabbath would be on Sunday, the first day of the week, rather than Saturday, the seventh? Seventh-Day Adventists and some other groups maintain that the Sabbath was changed by Constantine around A.D. 325 when he, the first Christian emperor of Rome, made the first day of the week into the legal Sabbath. Anyone who supposes that Constantine changed the Sabbath day makes an error, for the Christian record is that from the beginning the church recognized that the symbol of God's rest on the seventh day was fulfilled when Christ arose on the first. And Sunday represents in the fullest sense the rest of all Christ's people from the burden of their sin. Let us take a brief look at the record of the Sabbath:

1. Jesus rose from the dead on the first day of the week; he appeared to the women and to the disciples on their way to Emmaus on that day of resurrection.
2. On the following first day of the week he appeared to Thomas and the other disciples.
3. The Holy Spirit was poured out on the church on the day of Pentecost, the first day of the week, and so the church was founded on this day, and Acts reports that Christians assembled on the first day of the week. The word used in Acts is the word from which we get "synagogue"; they "synagogued" together on the first day of the week. Collection for the poor was made on the first day as well.
4. It was on the first day, "the Lord's Day," that John was in the Spirit and saw Christ, high and lifted up and mighty (Revelation 1:10).
5. In A.D.120, less than twenty-five years after John died, Barnabas, one of the early church fathers, wrote: "They kept the eighth day with joyfulness, the day in which Jesus rose from the dead." In A.D. 150 Justin Martyr recorded: "Sunday is the day on which we all hold our communion assem-

bly because Jesus Christ, our Savior, on the same
day arose from the dead."
6. In A.D. 194 Clement of Alexandria declared of the
   Christian: "He, in fulfillment of the precept according to the Gospel keeps the Lord's Day."
7. In about 200 Tertullian, another church father,
   added, "We solemnize the day after Saturday in
   contradiction to those who call that day their
   Sabbath [namely, the Jews]."

Beyond all this, do you suppose Constantine, who
legalized the day to keep the support of the Christians
who had helped him come to power, would have alienated those Christians by changing the day of their worship?

No, Sunday is the proper day for Christians to keep,
though those who meet to honor and worship the Lord
in Spirit and in truth will hardly be turned away from
his throne because they missed their appointment.
Still, the keeping of Sunday is the keeping of the biblical "Lord's Day," the day for remembering that God
created the world and rested therein, for Sabbath
comes from the Hebrew *Shabbot*, meaning "rest." We
further remember the Son's resurrection and the Holy
Spirit's outpouring, and we look forward to the Christian's ultimate fulfillment of the Sabbath: "There
remaineth therefore a rest to the people of God. For he
that is entered into his rest, he also hath ceased from
his own works, as God did from his" (Hebrews 4:9–10).

God's cycle of blessing

Yes, I think Sunday is a special day on God's weekly
calendar, but the Sabbath principles transcend a day
of the week, for they reflect an attitude of focused heart

and desire for God's company. God offers his presence lavishly. God's presence is not the problem. The problem is me. I am a fickle lover of my God. I ask for his nearness and begin to offer my adoration, and then I am distracted by some more immediate desire. I will get back to God as soon as there is time, and I know he will understand. No, I need the Sabbath desperately: It demands that my attention be pulled from other distractions and set upon my Lover and Savior and Lord. Were it not for the discipline of Sunday, I would have a great deal more difficulty glorifying God and enjoying him any day of the week.

Certainly I also would be poorer without one time to worship alongside those of my fellow lovers in Christ. For as hard as it is to get together one day each week, imagine what it would be like to have no one time when our assembly was called. I am convinced that keeping one day in seven expresses God's best desire for the well-being of the believing—and even the unbelieving—world.

Sunday blesses those who have never set their foot inside a place of worship. The very distinction that one family sleeps in and lounges in robes for brunch, while their neighbors get up early to shepherd the kids through breakfast and corral them in the car, remains a vital witness before the watching world. Assuming that the busy Sunday morning family walks their witness all week, and assuming they go to worship out of love rather than self-righteous religiosity, their children may complain, but they will remember. And the neighbors may politely joke about it, but they also will be impressed, respectful, and maybe a bit envious. Why? Because holding that one day of the week as special flows into the rest of the week. And walking a higher plane from Monday through Saturday makes Sunday a greater joy. Life becomes a revolving cycle of devotion for God, fueled by a day each week set aside for absorbing eternal values. This is no magic formula that makes all family problems disappear and all frustrations cease. Yet I know of few suicides, divorces, and irretrievably broken relationships with children among families that set aside Sunday as a day saved for eternity. Certainly crises happen in a world of imperfect, sinful people, but not often and almost never without hope of repair. It is one of Scripture's most precious promises:

> If thou turn away thy foot from the sabbath, from doing thy pleasure on my holy day; and call the sabbath a delight, the holy of the LORD, honourable; and shalt honour him, not doing thine own ways, nor finding thine own pleasure, nor speaking thine own words: Then shalt thou delight thyself in the LORD; and I will cause thee to ride upon the high places of the earth, and feed thee with the heritage of Jacob thy father: for the mouth of the LORD hath spoken it. [Isaiah 58:13–14]

The Sabbath principles

So what are the principles that empower the Sabbath? Chapter 20 of the *Westminster Confession of Faith* suggests several that deal specifically with worship and the Sabbath day. Here are some of them:

1. *Worship belongs to God.* It is his to demand by right, and he has revealed the pattern for the worship he desires us to follow.
2. *The pattern of acceptable worship directs itself to God,* to the exclusion of all else. Its focus sees only the lifting of the heart to fellowship with Father, Son, and Holy Spirit.

3. *True worship has a Mediator in Jesus the Christ* (see book 2, pp. 22–24). Other faiths may have an emotionally pleasing worshipful experience, but the only genuine worship occurs in the presence of the crucified and risen Lord.

4. *True worship revolves around communicating fellowship between people and their God* in prayer, the reading of Scriptures, sound preaching, listening with understanding and faith, singing with thanksgiving in the heart, and receiving God's sacraments as seals of his grace.

5. *Worship does not belong solely to a place or time.* Fellowship can take place anywhere and at any time, alone, in a family, or a congregation, under a roof or without one. We need not stand in a cathedral, nor face a Mecca.

6. *Yet God set aside a tithe of time each week* when he is to particularly have our attention, and that day is most appropriately Sunday.

7. *The Sabbath is a holy cessation, a set-apart stopping,* for which we should prepare our hearts during the rest of the week.

Standing apart in joy

Humankind has wandered long and far seeking these principles. The heart is unfilled without the blessed fellowship of God, without knowing once more the restoration of the communion Adam and Eve knew before the fall. One of the most incredible thoughts the mind can contemplate is that the majestic God who guides galaxies in their courses through the heavens desires to walk with us as well. I would that this thought could sink into my mind adequately. How thrilled you would be to receive an invitation to the

White House because the President wants to meet you. What if the Queen of England communicated with you that she desires the presence of your person and the fellowship of your company? Yet, what is that to fellowship with the Creator of the universe?

Why do multitudes of church members never know anything vaguely approaching the joy of this fellowship? Charles Spurgeon offered a parable in illustration:

Suppose that a great plague comes upon the city of London. The population is decimated, and every heart is filled with terror at the sight of death on every side. Now in the city dwells a man of noble lineage with his son, who is a wonderful physician. They determine to give themselves to reclaiming the sick. The son unbars the great front gate to their estate and makes his way into the dismal streets where piles of the dead and dying lie about. Finding those who still live, he picks them up in his arms and brings them back to his father's house, where gradually he uses his marvelous skill to restore them to wholeness. The father smiles benignly upon his son, in whom he has such great delight and who is exposing himself to grievous dangers by returning again and again to the city to bring back another victim.

Let us suppose that you are one of those lying in the street, contorted with pain. The virulent disease is making its way through your body. He picks you up tenderly in his arms and carries you back to the house. There he bends over you to begin his ministrations. You will never know anything of the fellowship of God unless you have experienced that healing balm that restores your life. Only in the house of this noble man and his healing son can you enter into an understanding of this great enterprise that is being accomplished. You allow him to touch your body, and you feel the health restored to your limbs. You begin to find that life once more pulses throughout your frame; you know restoration to health and soundness.

But even then you will not be able fully to enter into that fellowship. First, you must come to some sort of understanding of what is really happening around you. You must see that there is nothing in London, nothing indeed in all the world, that begins to compare in significance to the tremendous work going on in these rooms before your eyes. Day by day, as you watch the work of this great father and son, you become more impressed. You realize that this is the only hope of this town, and you enter sympathetically and understandingly into what they are doing. Yet you must go further to enter into fellowship. You must come to the place where you say timidly, "Sir, is it possible that such a one as I could have some small part in this great work that you are doing?"

You are given the task of carrying basins and bringing towels. You begin to understand more fully what is involved and to have a part in the fellowship and communion that goes on between these two, for it has become part of your life as well. Still, you are not ready to fully understand and enter into that fellowship until you come to that day when you say, "Sir, I want not only to have some small part, but I see that this is the only thing in life which is really worthwhile. I want to give my whole self over to it. I yield myself, body and soul. I want to go out and join your son in bringing in the ill. I want to expose myself to the dangers and even the taunts of those who do not understand. I will give even my life for this cause."

At that point you begin to enter in and understand the deep mystery of the fellowship of the father and his son.

One day in that great house you meet a young man who announces that he, too, is one of those who has been brought in and healed and restored and has been adopted into the family. You find out a little about him. He is dressed in a sporting way. He has a tennis racket under his arm, and he is on his way out the door. As he comes to the drawing room near the front door he peers in and says to the son, "How is it going with the plague today? How many was it this week? . . . Oh, that is splendid! I'm delighted to hear it. I'm on my way to the courts to have a game!" Would such a one as this ever be able to enter into the fellowship of the father and the son?

Or perhaps you meet another man, not nearly so frivolous and flippant as the first. He is dressed in a three-piece suit. His umbrella is under his arm. You find that he is on his way to the Board of Trade. "Well, you know, business has to go on even in the most difficult of times, and in times like these it is possible to make a good profit if one keeps his eyes open and his nose to the grind." He, too, stops by the drawing room, tips his hat to the father and son and says, "Glad to hear that the work is going well. I left a check on the table in the hallway to help continue the work. How is that poor soul there doing? My, he does look bad. But I must run along now. Business first." Can such a person enter into that mystery of fellowship between the father and the son? That will remain ever as alien to him as to someone from another planet.

The means and meaning of Sunday

Are you hungry for the sort of fellowship in Spurgeon's story? It does not begin with deciding to join up with the Son and his Father in their grand crusade. That would only be a works righteousness, without the soul depth of sanctification. Spurgeon saw that the belonging comes with feeling the soothing hands, of allowing the balm of the Physician to do its work, of convalescing in the house of God and getting to know intimately its layout and the ways of its triune Inhabitants, of growing to love the other servants of the house just because they are fellow survivors of the disease who also have been rescued from death on the streets.

That sort of relationship grows through a worship that flows like a river into the life of the individual and washes over all of the thoughts and doings of the week. And God established Sunday as one of the floodgates through which that river flows into our daily lives. The Word of God and the sacraments are special "means of grace" for God's empowering of our lives. Those means give Sunday's rest and communion special meaning as the Father's day of rest, the Son's day of redemption and resurrection, and the Holy Spirit's day of outpouring.

We remember the promise that there yet remains unto the children of God a Sabbath, a day of rest, the eternal rest that God has promised to all of those that trust in Him. So, Father, Son, and Holy Spirit—creation, resurrection, and eternal life—are symbolized in the concept of the Lord's Day, the Sabbath day.

Problems with knowing how to keep this day to the Lord are not new. In England, King James I, who commissioned the King James Bible, a few years later commissioned a book of sports. When this was published in 1618, to the consternation of many Christians, it encouraged all Englishmen to play sports on Sabbath afternoon. This was one of the final irritations that led a certain group of Christians to decide to leave the country altogether. The Pilgrims started departing the next year and in 1620 arrived in America.

It is interesting that, from the inception of America, the founders of our nation were concerned about the Lord's Day. The Pilgrims on the Mayflower were blown into Plymouth Harbor and landed on Clark's Island, across from the rock where they finally came ashore. When the storm lifted it was Sunday morning. They were delighted to see where they were. They had been at sea for months in crowded quarters. They were eager to rush across the bay, land, and get off the ship. They did not. Instead, the first thing they did was to honor the Sabbath day, to hold worship and praise God. On Monday morning they landed on Plymouth Rock.

In the early 1800s, some years after the founding of the United States, a wave of anti-Sabbath feeling swept the country, including the government. Someone got the idea of speeding the mails by operating on Sunday, and the law was passed that the postmaster would be replaced at any post office that was closed on Sunday. The Christians of Philadelphia were incensed at this action, and the city government voted to wage civil disobedience against what they considered an attack on their First Amendment freedoms. When the mail coach approached Philadelphia the driver found that a huge chain had been locked in place across the highway. All roads leading to the city were closed every Sabbath in defiance. Interesting, isn't it, that to this day the U.S. Postal Service is one of the few enterprises that does not operate on Sundays?

We see the turning of the Lord's Day into a frivolous day, forgetting that it is the *day of the Lord*, a day for worship and rejoicing in the Lord. The Sabbath should be different from other days. It shouldn't be simply given over to secular sports and business and work. We should not be rushing about, trying to get as much of the secular world in us as possible. What we pour into our Sabbath spills over into the rest of the week. The fourth commandment says we are not to work on the Sabbath; we are to cease our secular work for the week, and we are to turn our thoughts heavenward. Those who turn away from the Sabbath find their lives becoming more and more secularized, and their thoughts less and less stayed about the Lord. The Sabbath should be a "day of rest and gladness," as one hymn-writer puts it, and not a day of solemnity and sadness. In the past some Christians have been guilty of taking all the joy from it. Older people have told me that in childhood their Sabbath reading material was restricted to the Bible and theological books. I recall reading that a few centuries back a Scotsman was arrested for smiling on the Sabbath day! In the early church at one point it was considered improper to kneel while praying on Sunday. One could only stand in prayer on that day. That is not the dominant feeling of most in the early church, though. The *Didache*, a manual for teaching Christians in the early second century, saw the importance of joyful, thankful worship. Notice also the importance set on getting ready for worship by getting interpersonal reconciliations in order first:

> And on the Lord's own day gather yourselves together and break bread and give thanks, first confessing your transgressions, that your sacrifice may be pure. And let no man, having his dispute with his fellow, join your assembly until they have been reconciled, that your sacrifice may not be defiled; for this sacrifice it is that was spoken of by the Lord; In every place and at every time offer me a pure sacrifice; for I am a great king, saith the Lord, and my name is wonderful among the nations.

To observe the Sabbath properly we need to prepare ourselves for it. The *Didache's* instruction stressed one element Jesus said was important—so important that he said to leave the sacrifice on the altar and be reconciled (Matthew 5:24). Another issue involved in preparation is especially important today. In Old Testament times the day before the Sabbath was called "the day of preparation." You cannot observe the Sabbath without preparation. We need to purchase what needs to be purchased on the day of preparation, and not on the Lord's Day. Buying and selling was one of the reasons that God took the Hebrew people away into Babylonian captivity. In our great-grandparents' day Saturday was the special day of baking and cooking, so that little food preparation would be needed on Sunday. In many homes it gave a specially festive air to the day of preparation. The modern version of that practice often is going to a restaurant after church. That adds pressure to restaurant owners to take away the Sabbath day of their employees. More than one Christian store owner has complained that it is almost impossible to stay closed on Sundays, partly because of losing all of the Christian customers who do their shopping after church.

In giving to us the Sabbath, God has given to us a greater life. A medical study by Johns Hopkins Medical School found that men who attend church regularly have about one-half the chance of dying with a heart attack as those who do not. In the statistics 500 out of 100,000 who attend church regularly die with heart attacks; 900 out of 100,000 who do not attend church regularly die from heart attacks. If you stretch a rubber band but never let it relax, eventually it will lose its elasticity. And that is the way the human body reacts. The Sabbath day, properly exercised, adds a joy break to the cycle of life, a time of focusing off of self and onto those things for which we are created—to glorify God and to enjoy him. Little wonder the time of worship is also good for us.

The call of "Save Our Sunday" may seem a lost cause. Certainly Christians would not want to be so punctilious about it as were the Jews Jesus condemned for their lack of balance. The Jews observed 1521 laws covering every conceivable thing that might or might not be done on the Sabbath. A woman keeping those laws would not look in a mirror on the Sabbath because she might see a gray hair and be tempted to pull it out. Should she do so she would be carrying a burden. Such humorous laws were less funny to Jesus when he saw these hypocritical people refusing his right to heal. They were more worried about whether his disciples ate some grain from the field than they were to worship God in Spirit and in truth. As the *Westminster Confession* makes clear, the purpose of the Sabbath is the purpose of all of life—worship and fellowship—the floodgate through which enjoyment of God enters into all the week's life.

For those who perform works of necessity on Sunday, and for those who see no option but to fulfil employment demands on that day, the blessing of the Sabbath may still be found at other times. But this way is full of temptation to turn aside. And for those Christians who exemplify the Jews and fret about when the Sabbath will be over so they could get on with their lives, the blessing missed is costly. A great many earn the epitaph on a tombstone in France:

> "He was born a man,
> and died a grocer."

I can think of few sorrier ways for anyone to be remembered, but especially children of God in Jesus Christ, who are made to glorify and enjoy.

In that one day of God-centeredness, reminds the *Westminster Confession*, we find that all of our worship does indeed belong to God, that the pattern is God's to direct, and that the Mediator who truly leads each God-centered worship experience is Jesus Christ. The hours we spend communicating with fellow believers and our God in prayer, preaching, song, and sacrament bring us closest to what will be the highlight of heaven. For this reason if for no other, Sunday is a day saved for eternity. It is the holy cessation, the day for which we should long through the rest of the week. It has lost that place in our society. But the Sabbath is not kept in a society. It is kept in a heart—a heart saved for eternity.

The epitome of a Sabbath-keeper today is found in the beautiful story of Eric Liddell, the hero of the movie *Chariots of Fire*, who did one thing that has made him forever famous: He refused to run an Olympic race on Sunday. God blessed his stand. When he ran the alternative 400-meter race the next day he won the gold medal, although this was not his distance.

Another peculiarity in the story of Liddell tells us that his feelings about worship and the Sabbath were an extension of his view of life. Other runners were mystified by Liddell's unique sprinting style. He never looked where he was going. Instead, he burst from the starting gates and around the lane with his eyes fixed upward at the sky. When another runner tripped into his lane in one big race there was a terrible collision because Liddell had no thought of anyone being in his path. He flung himself forward as if there were no tomorrow and looked straight to the sky where his tomorrow lay. When the Japanese invaded China and interned missionary Liddell in a prison camp he exhausted himself in service until a disease took his life. The man whose courage stood until the last was strengthened by a cycle of life that revolved around looking skyward to glorify God and to enjoy him forever. The Sabbath lifted his eyes to eternity.

What makes relationships whole in Christ?

A lawful oath is a part of religious worship, wherein, upon just occasion, the person swearing solemnly calleth God to witness what he asserteth or promiseth; and to judge him according to the truth or falsehood of what he sweareth. . . . It is the duty of the people to pray for magistrates, to honor their persons, to pay them tribute and other dues, to obey their lawful commands, and to be subject to their authority, for conscience' sake. . . . Marriage was ordained for the mutual help of husband and wife; for the increase of mankind with a legitimate issue, and of the Church with an holy seed; and for preventing of uncleanness. [Westminster Confession of Faith, chapters 22–24]

5

Sand in the Shoes

We now run together pieces of three chapters of the *Westminster Confession of Faith*. Chapter 22 covers lawful oaths and vows, chapter 23 the civil magistrate, and chapter 24, marriage and divorce. A common thread runs through this section, as the writers of the *Confession* summarize all that the Scriptures say about relationships among people. We might have added the sections on the church (chapters 25 and 26), but those have some special considerations we will want to look at. These brief statements do not seem as edifying as other parts of the Westminster documents, with reason: Since the fall, interpersonal relations have woven a web of pain. To deal with it all requires either an encyclopedia or a shopping list.

Issues related to the Christian and government have received some discussion above, so now we will focus on marriage as the most intricate part of the relationship web, keeping in mind that some principles apply to obligations with other people and even with government. The closer you get to the marriage covenant, the more you see that it is both a unique bond, and the template for other bonds. Martin Luther said that when he looked at the command to love his neighbor as himself he thought first of Katie Luther. She was, after all, his closest neighbor.

The law of love

It strikes me that the *Confession* most clearly says two things about relationships with our neighbors (those as close as a spouse and as far off as an opponent in political or philosophical warfare). One teaching is that our relationships relate to worship. How we treat others reflects how we treat God. Jesus said this in his answer about the greatest commandment of the law:

> Thou shalt love the Lord thy God with all thy heart, and with all thy soul, and with all thy mind. This is the first and great com-

> *Let love be without dissimulation [deception]. Abhor that which is evil; cleave to that which is good. Be kindly affectioned one to another with brotherly love; in honour preferring one another.* [Romans 12:9–10]

mandment. And the second is like unto it, Thou shalt love thy neighbour as thyself. [Matthew 22:37–39]

According to Matthew 6:12, 14–15, even God's forgiveness of us depends on how we forgive others.

The second teaching is that relationships do not come easy. Sinful people are selfish. We try to weasel out of obligations, and obligations are involved in relationships, whether an obligation to pray for my enemy, to obey my ruler, or to love my wife sacrificially. The *Westminster Confession* chapter on marriage makes the interesting statement about divorce: Human corruption is such that we are "apt to study arguments, unduly to put asunder those whom God hath joined together in marriage." In other words, we usually come up with an excuse to justify breaking obligations that become too much work. Things haven't changed all that much since the 1640s.

Human nature hasn't changed, but society certainly has. The great Roman Empire began as a lowly nation with strong moral values but grew steadily in strength and power until its might eclipsed the greatest grandeur ever achieved by Babylon, Assyria, or Egypt. Many books have been written on that subject, but one reason often overlooked is that for the first 500 years of Rome's existence there was recorded one divorce. Then, at the zenith of its glory, its people became decadent and they relaxed this extraordinary value placed on stable families. In the first century it was said that Roman women of the upper class changed husbands as often as they changed hairstyles. Waves of dissolution crashed upon the Empire as her foundation gave way. Finally hordes of barbarians from the north moved in to finish off a society that already had died within. There were other reasons for the fall of Rome, but few historians would deny that family disintegration was a major influence.

After the Puritan population began growing in America, even though not all the immigrants were Puritans or even Christians, the average number of divorces was one-third of one divorce per year. This was true when the colonial population reached 70,000. By the mid-1700s the divorce rate had climbed to one in 500 marriages. By 1812 there was one divorce for every 110 marriages. This slow climb continued until World War II. A book published during the war claimed that society was relaxing its attitudes toward marriage, and the author predicted an alarming increase in the number of divorces that bode ill for the future of American society. In the year that he wrote, divorces in the U.S. could be counted in the tens of thousands. His worst fears came to pass: There were 395,000 divorces in 1959. By 1965 the annual rate was 479,000. By 1977 the number of divorces had grown to over 1 million a year and in 1979 to 1.8 million a year. Today, depending on the part of the country, the number of divorces equals or exceeds one-half the number of marriages. This doesn't include the number of short-term live-in relationships that begin and end at the whim of the participants. The worst disaster has befallen the black family, which in the urban impoverished areas has virtually ceased to exist. More than two-thirds of all black children today are born into one-parent homes. Families receiving support through welfare, especially Aid to Families with Dependent Children (AFDC), cannot even afford to remain married. They qualify for benefits only if the father is missing. This is a tragic commentary of terrifying proportions. The attitude toward marriage relationships in particular, and all other relationships as a result, makes the standards of the *Westminster Confession* seem unreachable. I would also suggest one statistic that to me is most devastating in its implications: The divorce rate among professing Christians is only slightly lower than that for the surrounding society in any given area.

Innumerable books, classes, and counseling programs have been designed to help troubled marriages. Some are extremely good, but most are like the ambulance at the bottom of the cliff after the car has gone off the road and over the side of the mountain. Surely the church and the Word of God have something to say to those who have made a wreck of their marriages. Divorce is not the unpardonable sin. The grace of God is real. But instead of becoming the ambulances and hearses at the bottom, wouldn't it be better to build a safety rail around the top of the cliff to prevent tragedies? We need to realize what God thinks about the dissolution of the family unit, when men do separate what God has joined together. "I hate divorce," says the LORD God of Israel (Malachi 2:16 NIV).

The law God gave to Old Testament Israel makes two specific statements about marriage and divorce, in Deuteronomy 22 and 24. The former deals with a married person caught in the act of adultery. The penalty for adultery was death. When the Romans took away from the Jews the power of capital punishment, it was recognized that adultery destroyed the marital bond and laid grounds for divorce. Everyone agreed on this, but were there other grounds? Moses says in Deuteronomy 24 that a husband could put away his wife if he found "some uncleanness" in her. That is rather vague, so the Jewish teachers of the law sought to interpret this allowance, developing two schools of thought. The teacher Shammai led the strict interpretation that only uncleanness of a gross character would be grounds for a divorce. Another teacher, Hillel, guided the party that believed anything unseemly "in the eyes of the husband" would be a grounds. It was said that if a husband was not pleased with the way his wife cooked his eggs or combed her hair he could give her a writing of divorcement and put her away. Hillel is much more famous than Shammai. The *Westminster Confession* statement about human corruption reveals the secret of Hillel's popularity.

The Pharisees tried to pit Christ against one or the other of these schools, thinking to divide Jesus' fol-

lowers. But Christ was never competing in a personality contest. He ignored the views of both Hillel and
Shammai and went back beyond the Mosaic law to the
purpose of marriage itself:

> Have ye not read, that he which made them at the
> beginning made them male and female, and said, For
> this cause shall a man leave father and mother, and
> shall cleave to his wife: and they twain shall be one
> flesh? Wherefore they are no more twain, but one flesh.
> What therefore God hath joined together, let not man
> put asunder. [Matthew 19:4–6]

Inherent in Christ's response is the implication that
marriage is not a fifty-fifty partnership. It is not a true
partnership at all, though that is a helpful metaphor.
Marriage is a relationship—the closest relationship
that any two people can know in this world. A
husband and wife are one flesh. In this statement
Jesus offered the secret to a happy marriage and the
challenge to make a marriage work in an unfriendly
culture: To men Jesus says, "Your wife is you"; to
women he says, "Your husband is you." Two have
become one flesh.

The sand of criticism and disinterest

Too often the marriage partnership suffers from the
same woe as did a man who walked across the North
American continent on foot. When he got to California,
reporters questioned him about his travels. He was
asked if he had ever felt that he wouldn't make it. "Yes,
many times," he replied.

What had almost defeated him? Well, it wasn't the
traffic of the big cities or the screeching of brakes and

honking of horns. It wasn't even the interminable prairie of the Midwest that seemed to stretch on and on forever, nor the blazing sun over the hot Western desert. It wasn't even the snow-capped Rocky Mountains.

"What almost defeated me over and over again was the sand in my shoes."

It is this unheralded, seldom-discussed sand in the shoes that underlies some of the more spectacular reasons for marital failure. Much of this "sand in the shoes" is the abrasive sand of criticism, building up self by tearing down another in ever so small ways. Each grain seems insignificant, but they soon collect in very uncomfortable places.

This problem has its source in the parent-child relationship. A baby is born and lies in its crib, kicking its legs, waving its arms, and crying out for its parents. It is doing the one thing that comes naturally to every baby—seeking attention and looking for recognition. Soon the little one learns to talk: "Mommy, look! Look, Daddy! It's a rabbit! I drew it myself! Isn't it good, Daddy?" The child is expressing a need for acceptance and recognition that will be expressed over and over again throughout life. Is there really a basic difference between a child holding up a crayon picture, a college student laboring into the night for all A's, or Napoleon marching on Waterloo? The quest is for recognition, the search for acceptance by others.

But instead of acceptance little Johnny comes toddling out of the kitchen with his orangeade and it goes splat over the carpet. Then, like all Gaul, Johnny is divided into three parts: "You've done it again! How many times have I told you? Every time you pick up something you drop it. You are a numskull! Haven't you any sense at all? How are you ever going to get through school? You'll never amount to anything!" If a guest had spilled that drink mother would have dismissed it with the wave of a hand: "Oh, it's nothing at all. I'll just wipe it up later. I do it all the time myself."

By the time Johnny and Mary grow up, their feet have been worn to a bloody pulp by the sand in their shoes. But they hope to find a loving, soothing, comforting, accepting partner who will heal the wounds. They want someone who will see something worthwhile in them, because they may still suspect that there is something in them that is lovable. At last they find just such a person. They get married and suddenly in alarm make the sad discovery that their partner is not so perfect as they thought. This person has some good points, but those bad points have got to go. Now one or both newlyweds makes the colossal mistake of supposing that the best way to magnify the good and get rid of the bad is to tell their spouse about the bad ones. If the husband or wife is told often and loudly enough, surely he or she will correct them and become ideal. Unfortunately, it seldom occurs to anyone to magnify the good points before all the world and let the bad points take care of themselves. If it ever did, the bad would likely shrivel away from lack of nurture.

Instead, the day comes when the husband or wife just suddenly isn't there any longer. "What does my husband see in that woman? She's older and uglier than I am. She must be blinder, too, if she thinks there is something nice about him! Can that woman who has run off with my husband be that dumb? And why would he leave me for her?"

While having lunch in a restaurant I noticed a couple sitting at the next table. They were not yet 35 years old, but they looked like they had been married for about 275 years. They never said one word to each other during the hour that I sat there and had lunch. Their chins were down on the table, and they looked like misery incarnate. I wondered what had brought this fine looking young couple to this abject state. After lots of years of counseling I suspect it was something like this:

"Honey, how do you like my new rose bush? It's blooming now. Aren't those roses beautiful?" But instead of sharing her enthusiasm he makes a grunting assent and wanders off. After a few encounters she realizes that the man who had a great fondness for roses when they were engaged now doesn't have any interest whatsoever in them or the time and energy she has spent growing them.

During the game of the week the scene changes: "Did you see that pass? Wow, 95 yards and in for a touchdown!"

"Yeah; but can't you do anything but sit there all day and watch football?"

Then the wife wants to share the beautiful poem she has found in a book.

"Poetry! I can't stand poetry. Why can't they write so you can understand what they're talking about?"

"I thought you liked poetry. You used to send me those . . . "

"Oh, I copied them off greeting cards."

Scratch roses. Scratch football. Scratch poetry. Scratch philosophy. Soon mealtimes become very quiet. Everything that either of them is really interested in has been put down by the other, verbally, by tone of voice, inference, sarcasm, rejection, or disinterested attitude. Their interests are boring. They are not worthwhile. They are unworthy of interest or importance. How foolish can we be that we create our own misery and then sit back and lament the sand in the shoes. The wise husband or wife realizes that a marriage license should be a hunting license, a license to seek virtue and goodness.

Whatsoever things are true, whatsoever things are honest, whatsoever things are just, whatsoever things are pure, whatsoever things are lovely, whatsoever things are of good report; if there be any virtue, and if there be any praise, think on these things. [Philippians 4:8]

If you want whole relationships with your spouse, your children, your boss, your best friend, your worst enemy, your brother or sister in Christ, that practical advice is the best place to start. Pour out the sand of devaluing the other person, the abrasive criticism and the thoughtless disinterest. Wives, what does your husband like that you could not care less about? Husbands, what does your wife like that you can't stand? The marriage covenant obligation demands that you learn enough about those interests to be able to support your partner and make him or her feel worthwhile. You may be amazed to find out that there really is something valuable in that interest, but the important thing is to communicate that you care.

The sand of unforgiveness

Another sandbox in a relationship is unforgiveness. Forgiveness is absolutely vital to wholeness in a sinful world, for we each have lots of occasions when we need to forgive—and more times when we need to be forgiven. Forgiveness in Christian living is not an option. No obligation more clearly connects with what God has done for us and expects us to mirror with one another. God forgave when it was neither expedient nor easy. If I avoid this aspect of loving neighbor as self I stand face-to-face with a bleeding figure writhing on a cross in my place.

But they and our fathers dealt proudly, and hardened their necks, and hearkened not to thy commandments, And refused to obey, neither were mindful of thy wonders that thou didst among them; but hardened their necks, and in their rebellion appointed a captain to return to their bondage: but thou art a God ready to pardon, gracious and merciful, slow to anger, and of great kindness, and forsookest them not. [Nehemiah 9:16–17]

For if, when we were enemies, we were reconciled to God by the death of his Son, much more, being reconciled, we shall be saved by his life. [Romans 5:10]

Who hath delivered us from the power of darkness, and hath translated us into the kingdom of his dear Son: in whom we have redemption through his blood, even the forgiveness of sins. [Colossians 1:13–14]

If we confess our sins, he is faithful and just to forgive us our sins, and to cleanse us from all unrighteousness. [1 John 1:9]

And we are compelled by the blood of Christ to go and do likewise.

After this manner therefore pray ye: Our Father which art in heaven, Hallowed be thy name. . . . And forgive us our debts, as we forgive our debtors. . . . For if ye forgive men their trespasses, your heavenly Father will also forgive you: But if ye forgive not men their trespasses, neither will your Father forgive your trespasses. [Matthew 6:9–15]

Judge not, and ye shall not be judged: condemn not, and ye shall not be condemned: forgive, and ye shall be forgiven. [Luke 6:37; see also Matthew 7:1]

And be ye kind one to another, tenderhearted, forgiving one another, even as God for Christ's sake hath forgiven you. [Ephesians 4:32]

Like many of the Lord's commands, this one is good for me. I need to forgive, for I need to be forgiven. This need exists in any human-to-human relationship, the closer the relationship the greater the need. In the marriage relationship I need to forgive, and I need to be forgiven, on a number of different levels. It is part of loving my closest neighbor as myself. In fact, according to Genesis, it *is* loving myself, if a husband and wife are one flesh.

The forgiving process may become complicated. People sometimes have trouble loving and forgiving others because they have the same difficulty with themselves. If we are Christians, of course, this should never be. We stand forgiven on the blood of Jesus Christ, and we have no right to withhold what God has personally given. In reality our neuroses and defense mechanisms can still get in the way, so that we do not feel forgiven, perhaps do not even wish to forgive ourselves for some reason, and so lack the desire to love and forgive others. "The heart is deceitful above all things, and desperately wicked: who can know it?" says God through the Prophet Jeremiah (17:9).

Thankfully, One does understand it, and it is his Spirit within us that empowers us to love the unlovely—even in ourselves. Forgiveness of others begins in self-awareness, of laying out our fears and feelings before the Lord, admitting our weakness, and asking his help. It may be that we have to begin by confessing to the Lord that we do not feel forgiving, do not feel forgiven, even though emotionally we know that we must forgive and are forgiven. If you go through these bitterly conflicting emotions, confess them and begin praying with all your heart for the one toward whom you feel them. Pray confessing that this love must come from the will and not from the emotions. Pray for that person's blessing, admitting that at the moment you don't really want it. If you do this you will begin to change. You cannot pray for someone, laying aside pretense, and remain an enemy. Jeremiah 17:14 goes on to make a wonderful promise, even in the midst of a deceitful heart: "Heal me, O LORD, and I shall be healed; save me, and I shall be saved: for thou art my praise." If you have broken relationships with anyone, and especially with your wife, the first step toward forgiveness and wholeness comes with praising God. He is the Source of wholeness, and when I center my thoughts on him I take them off the hurt and accept his healing touch.

Something else must be said about forgiving in that most intimate of relationships, the marriage. It is possible to forgive and love the adulterer, or a violent physical or sexual abuser, even when it is proper to end the marriage. God does not call a wife or a husband to undergo personal danger and torment and harm to children. The Bible allows but never *demands* that we divorce the marriage partner who commits adultery. Marriages can survive betrayal in glorious victory. The man or woman who allows a spouse to continue in ongoing or multiple adultery, however, should seek qualified Christian counsel, for the reason may have less to do with love than some unhealthy dependence. Still, the spouse who does have biblical grounds and seeks divorce does not have grounds for continual bitterness and hatred. That is neither personally healthy nor sanctifying, and it certainly does not honor God.

Forgiveness and judging

Thankfully, most of the needs for forgiveness are not so extreme, and so forgiveness is more a matter of sitting down by the way to empty the shoes of a little sand. I would not make light of these routine forgivenesses, for they are vitally important to keeping a marriage on track. The old movie platitude notwithstanding, "Love means saying you are sorry," and meaning it. And love means accepting that apology when it is given, even if the habit that seems so obnoxious doesn't disappear overnight. The wise wife or husband looks for the best in a spouse, realistically admits and discusses the flaws, but stresses that acceptance and love transcend bad habits and mistakes and weaknesses. This is the pattern of forgiveness God shows to us, and we act most like our Father when we model his forgiveness: "Yet now hath he reconciled In the body of his flesh through death, to present you holy and unblameable and unreproveable in his sight" (Colossians 1:21b-22).

Suppose your husband has a serious problem with forgetting to pick up his clothes from the middle of the floor. Suppose your wife simply cannot brush her teeth without leaving a glob of toothpaste in the sink. How does one deal with these small but real annoyances without the critical spirit that henpecks and pours sand in the shoes? These flaws can shift the focus of the relationship until one no longer sees the good points. The glaring faults seem designed by the boorish spouse to make your life miserable. It should be such a simple thing for your spouse to change, but no matter how many times you remind, criticize, and harp, the actions seem to continue. In fact the husband or wife now becomes more sullen and defensive. Perhaps the one behavior changes. He begins to pick up his clothes. But a new tension, almost a power struggle for control, has begun.

A law of relationships is at work that someone will become whatever you say he or she is. The child who is called worthless and a failure will unconsciously meet that expectation. A child with the same level of intelligence and native ability that is continually encouraged and seen as worthwhile will tend to rise to the level of the confidence that has been expressed. Similarly, if a wife is continually disregarded and told she is a lazy slob who lies around the house all day, then what she does is obviously unappreciated. In fact, she will likely come to agree with that assessment and lose the drive to manage the home and children well. Why should she? The husband who is told he is a bum and will never amount to anything will fill that expectation. This is one of the reasons why all the great "wars on poverty" have only deepened the cycle of failure. The recipients are tagged, perceived, and labeled to be failures who will perpetually live on the dole. It is one reason successful rehabilitation will never be achieved within the prison system. The institutionalized individual almost inevitably comes to identify himself or herself with the Department of Corrections number they carry.

The Scriptures speak plainly about these matters, though we have tended to think the instruction idealistic. Jesus said:

> Judge not, that ye be not judged. For with what judgment ye judge, ye shall be judged: and with what measure ye mete, it shall be measured to you again. [Matthew 7:1–2]

Many believe he really did not mean *that* or they feel that somehow we can escape the inevitable consequences of the laws involved there. However, in the physical world we have been told that for every action there is an equal and opposite reaction. Jesus tells us that the same thing exists in the moral and spiritual realms. The Greek words might better be translated, "Do not continually be judging. Do not make this the way of your life." One of the problems of denying forgiveness and fault-finding is that, just as you blind yourself to your spouse's good points, so you blind your spouse to your own good points. I defy you to continually express what is wrong with your spouse and then expect him or her to deepen in love and admiration for you. Soon both of you will see nothing good, and you will sit before some marriage counselor as Mr. and Mrs. Frankenstein in one another's eyes.

Carrying one another's burdens

Christ is the Friend of sinners. The accuser is the Devil. In relationships we can mirror the love of God's forgiveness in Christ or the judgmental accusations of Satan. Certainly we can find and express fault with someone. Jesus was talking about habitual fault-finding of anyone, and especially that person with whom we are one flesh or our children. Paul gives a wise perspective in Galatians 6:1–2. Though spoken to the church it applies well to the marriage and all relationships with Christians. In fact, it is the obligation of relationships in Christ:

> Brethren, if a man be overtaken in a fault, ye which are spiritual, restore such an one in the spirit of meekness; considering thyself, lest thou also be tempted. Bear ye one another's burdens, and so fulfil the law of Christ.

This means that, instead of pecking away at faults, we go to the person in a spirit of meekness, after first considering our own weaknesses, and faults, and spiritual relationship with God. We go not to demolish but to restore—actually to help the person carry the burden of that habit or fault, or some underlying issue that may be beneath the outward problem. Criticism must be approached as one approaches a dangerous explosive, with fear and trepidation. And it must never be used without accompanying notices of what is good, meaningful, and worthwhile in the person's life. The goal must be to fulfil the law of Christ, the goal of self-sacrificing, supportive love.

I am certain you will enrich your marriage, and remove the painful sand from the shoes of your life together, by putting Galatians 6:1 into practice in the context of Philippians 4:8. The secret is to look for the good in the other person, always striving to think about what is true, noble, right, pure, lovely, admirable, excellent, and praiseworthy in the life of another. What would happen if you took time to sit down with your spouse and participate or learn about something that he or she enjoys and is good at? What would happen if you sought opportunities to celebrate some little victory in his or her life or took a moment to pray with your spouse especially about some tension or problem? I am certain you would enrich your own marriage. You would bless your home, your children, your grandchildren. Love would blossom in your home. And on a different level those same techniques will bless your friends, coworkers, and even the person you can't stand.

The following quotation is excerpted from a poem from the most prolific author of all time: "anonymous." Maybe a reader will identify its original author. I have cherished its truths, and I hope you will be able to sign your name to both sides of its story, and thus fulfil the obligation of the law of love for neighbor as for self:

> I love you,
> Not only for what you are,

But for what I am
When I am with you.

I love you,
Not only for what
You have made of yourself,
But for what
You are making of me.

I love you,
for putting your hand
Into my heaped-up heart
And passing over
All the foolish, weak things
That you can't help
Dimly seeing there,
And for drawing out
Into the Light
All the beautiful belongings
that no one else had looked
Quite far enough to find.

I love you,
Because you are helping me
To make of the lumber
Of my life
Not a tavern
But a temple;
Out of the works
Of my every day
Not a reproach
But a song.

What makes relationships whole in Christ?

The catholic or universal Church, which is invisible, consists of the whole number of the elect, that have been, are, or shall be gathered into one, under Christ the head thereof; and is the spouse, the body, the fullness of him that filleth all in all. [Westminster Confession of Faith, chapter 25]

6

Holy, Catholic Church

A little boy was busily building something out in the backyard. Observing the activity, his father went out to discover what was taking place and asked, "What are you building, son?"

"Shh! Shh! I'm building a church and we must be very quiet."

Eager to encourage this sense of reverence in his son, the father bent down and whispered, "And just why must we be so quiet in church, son?"

"Because all the people are asleep," came the whispered reply.

The New England Puritans knew how to deal with sleepers. Ushers were equipped with long poles. To the end of the pole was affixed a long and very sharp needle. John Wesley also was adept at handling sleepy congregations. One day he looked down from the pulpit at a snoozing man and stopped right in the middle of his sentence. Silence pervaded the room. Then Wesley cried out, "FIRE! FIRE!" The slumbering man leaped to his feet in surprise and asked, "Where?" Wesley answered, "In hell, man, for those who sleep under the gospel."

Building his church

I am not all that bothered that some sleep in church; my concern is that more sleep in bed because they don't bother to come at all, even among those who call themselves Christians. One Lutheran minister listed in his bulletin some reasons "Why I don't go to the movies:

1. My parents made me go when I was a child.
2. No one speaks to me when I am there.
3. Because they always ask for money.
4. Because the manager never visits me at home.
5. Because the people who do go don't live according to what the movies teach."

In spite of all the criticism, much of it as ridiculous as this, the church has continued to grow. Jesus guaranteed that the gates of hell would not prevail against it. He said, "I will build my church." He gave us the first lesson in church building while teaching his circle of disciples one day. He began with a question, "Who do people say the Son of Man is?" There were some popular and very complimentary answers to

> *And there came unto me one of the seven angels which had the seven vials full of the seven last plagues, and talked with me, saying, Come hither, I will shew thee the bride, the Lamb's wife.*
> [Revelation 21:9]

that question, for Jesus was loved by all except the religious leaders:

> Some say that thou art John the Baptist: some, Elias; and others, Jeremias, or one of the prophets. He saith unto them, But whom say ye that I am? And Simon Peter answered and said, Thou art the Christ, the Son of the living God. [Matthew 16:14–16]

Jesus built his church, not upon the foundation of those who said and thought nice things about him, but upon the rock of the profession of faith that Peter first made that Jesus Christ is the divine Redeemer, Savior and Lord. That true church of Jesus Christ continues to grow. To watch television or read most secular media publications, one would suppose that the church has ceased to exist or is hopelessly fossilized and led by contemptible sexual perverts and social misfits. In fact, if you add up all the attendance figures from every game of professional sports played throughout the year in the United States and Canada, you will not come close to the total number of people who attend church. The church is the largest institution that has ever existed. More than 1.35 billion today profess faith in Christ at least nominally, and at the present rate of growth that number will reach 5 billion in another century if the Lord does not return. The church today is growing faster than the rate of population growth. That growth is not apparent to us because the historic denominations in the historically Christian West have overwhelmingly turned from the historic faith, and they are declining in membership. In the third world the number who share Peter's confession and gather into the universal body of Christ is growing at a phenomenal rate.

The purpose of the church

Despite the growth and all that Scripture says about this wondrous organization and its members, a lot of misunderstanding and misinformation exists about the church. Those reasons the minister came up with for not going to church bring to mind the basic question of why we *should* go to church. Surely we can worship God by ourselves, without a fancy building, a piano or organ, a preacher, and a lot of people. Yes, we can, but will we? Even in the first-century church, some were trying to follow Christ without the gathering of his people. The writer of the Book of Hebrews cautioned us not to follow their example. Why? Because we need to encourage one another (Hebrews 10:25). As sinful human beings we need to be encouraged and strengthened. We need to be chastened and disciplined. We need teaching and fellowship. We need to be responsible for and to other brothers and sisters. We need to be prepared for works of service. We need to be matured so we will no longer be tossed back and forth by the waves and blown here and there by every wind of teaching (Ephesians 4:14–16).

All of these are purposes of the church, but not the greatest purpose. The purpose of the church is to proclaim that Jesus is Lord. God could do all of his works by other means. But he has chosen to endow the bride of Christ with the greatest of all tasks, the commission of calling all the world to praise him forever.

This purpose empowers Evangelism Explosion and other movements that seek to invite the whole world to faith in Jesus Christ. I believe the church has the greatest purpose of any institution in all the world—a cosmic purpose established under cosmic authority. Jesus said:

All power is given unto me in heaven and in earth. Go ye therefore, and teach all nations, baptizing them in the name of the Father, and of the Son, and of the Holy Ghost: Teaching them to observe all things whatsoever I have commanded you: and, lo, I am with you alway, even unto the end of the world. [Matthew 28:18b–20]

It is the purpose of the church to say that "Jesus is Lord" by the way we live and worship before him. But we can't adequately say that Jesus is Lord if we stay cooped up in our little Christian ghetto. Charles Van Engen makes this point well in a book entitled *God's Missionary People: Rethinking the Purpose of the Local Church.* At one point he relates that to say "Jesus is Lord" means "Jesus is Lord of the world." The church can only do that if it is going out into the world. Writes Van Engen:

The Church of Jesus Christ exists when people confess with their mouth and believe in their heart that Jesus is Lord—Lord of the Church, of all people, and of all creation. Through this confession the Church emerges to become what it is, the missionary fellowship of disciples of the Lord Jesus Christ.

Only in the church are we endowed with the authority of God and the promise of Christ's presence to the end of the age. We are called to go into all the world and preach the gospel to all creation (Mark 16:15). Ours is not the work of saving the world or righting all wrongs. Ours is the job to be Christ's ambassadors, agents of reconciliation.

Holy and catholic, visible and invisible

The essential information we need to understand about the church is given to us in chapters 25 and 26 of the

Westminster Confession of Faith, of which we have copied the theme quotation for this chapter. From those two chapters we can develop a list of statements about what the church is and is not:

The catholic church

A lot of confusion has arisen among Protestants when they repeat in the *Apostles' Creed* that they believe in "a holy catholic church." The word *catholic* comes from two Greek words, *kata*, meaning "according to," and *holios*, meaning "the whole." *Catholic* means "according to the whole" or "universal." This universality distinguishes the church from the boundaries of our own parochial denominations. Some Christians who suppose that the church is no larger than their own rigid confession are going to be utterly amazed to count God's people when they get to heaven. Christians who understand Scripture should plan to throw away the labels and get to know folks from every communion who have trusted in Jesus Christ, who have repented of their sins, and who have received him as Lord and Savior.

The one Head of the church

Jesus Christ is the Lord of the church. In fact the Bible uses the beautiful analogy of Christ as our Husband, and we his bride, made chaste and pure—holy. The church is holy because it is called out of the world and set apart unto God. The word *holy* has two meanings in Scripture: (1) set aside for the worship and service of God; (2) cleansed and purified. Those who are truly part of the church find that their hearts are being sanctified and cleansed as they are prepared for the day when they shall bear no spot or blemish. The church is a long way from being perfect, but it is in the process of being cleansed by its Head. Human leaders are only servants in that process. There is room for only one true Head, and that is the Bridegroom.

The fulness of the Lord

The *Confession* says that the church "is the fulness of him who fills everything in every way." What does that mean? Colossians 1:16–20 makes an important connection between the being of God, the work of Christ, and the being of God's people:

> For by him were all things created. . . . And he is before all things, and by him all things consist. And he is the head of the body, the church: who is the beginning, the firstborn from the dead; that in all things he might have the preeminence. For it pleased the Father that in him should all fulness dwell; and, having made peace through the blood of his cross, by him to reconcile all things unto himself; by him, I say, whether they be things in earth, or things in heaven.

Paul writes that Christ's death and resurrection are an extension of his work as God, a work that began in creation, continued in God's providential control of creation, and climaxed in the work on the cross. Through the atonement God is reconciling all creation under Jesus Christ as God. That reconciliation preeminently includes bringing people into God's kingdom under Christ's headship—by way of the church. The church represents all the human race before God. The church is, says Peter, quoting the Old Testament description of Israel, a royal priesthood and a holy nation of people belonging to God (1 Peter 2:5). The church is a priesthood that represents the human race before God.

The fulness of Christ makes us responsible as salt and light, witness and intercessor before the Father. Christ sits in power and authority and glory in heaven and no longer visibly stands in the marketplace of humankind. Instead he has given to the world a Holy Spirit-empowered body to be his ambassador. We are the visible sign of Christ's kingship. That surely makes the church the most important institution that has ever existed for the good of the world. We are to stand as Jesus would stand if he were here. We will stand this watch on the ramparts until he comes to relieve us.

Inclusive and exclusive

"The church is the body of those who profess the true religion, together with their children." That statement makes a couple of points that have become fairly unpopular. First, we may be an inclusive body in urging all the world to be reconciled to God (see 2 Corinthians 5:11–21), but we are quite exclusive in demanding that our body only includes those who repent and place their faith in Jesus Christ as the Son of God, born of a virgin, suffered under Pontius Pilate, crucified, dead, buried, and arisen to sit at the right hand of God in power. The church is a body built upon a confession. Our belief has content. We teach that only one way takes sinful human beings to God.

Second, the church extends beyond those who fully understand and accept that true religion in that it takes in our children. We stand in a covenantal relationship that includes those too young to make a faith commitment on their own. They are holy through their parents. At some point they will have to make that commitment for themselves, but meanwhile they enjoy the nurture of God's family. For this reason a congregation shoulders much of the burden of praying for, guiding, and modeling Christ before the children of fellow members. No Christian is childless.

The ministry of the Word

God uses the church to gather and perfect the saints. We have the ministry of the Word of God. We have the ministry of the sacraments of baptism and the Lord's Supper. That means, among other things, that we are ministers to others, we are called to gather saints in evangelism and help disciple them, and we are also among those being gathered and discipled. In the church the Christian works both sides of the work of ministry. God gave us in Christ apostles, prophets, evangelists, pastors, and teachers (Ephesians 4:11) as we have needed them to disciple believers and win the lost. According to the *Confession*, God "doth by his own presence and Spirit, according to his promise, make them effectual thereunto." The church is a tool God uses to work his grace in the world and in my individual heart.

The invisible church

The true church is not the same as the organized church, but organization still is God's directive for us. This is to say that there exists a *visible* and an *invisible* body of Christ. The *Larger Catechism* sets the distinguishing marks of the visible, organized church, and the invisible, organic church.

What is the visible church? The visible church is a society made up of all such as in all ages and places of the world do profess the true religion, and of their children.

What is the invisible church? The invisible church is the whole number of the elect that have been, are, or shall be gathered into one under Christ the head.

When God led about 2 million descendants of Jacob out of Egypt he slowly organized them under judges, teachers, priests, clans, and families. At the end of the forty years in the wilderness the people were further organized into an army and then into provinces and cities as they made a place for themselves in the land. This was a visibly organized people, called out from the rest of the nations as holy before him. In a real sense this was a visible church, organized around goals of praise, worship, and sanctified life. Membership in the visible body was not restricted to the direct descendants of Abraham, for Scripture records that many other people besides the Hebrews joined the Exodus. They too wanted to be free from bondage and they could see the miraculous ways in which God was blessing this people. At no time does Moses distinguish between the ethnic descendants of the Patriarchs and these recent converts. Israel was not a racial designation, but a faith designation identified by a visible structure.

There also was a visible sign of membership that identified both the Jews and their children. Before going into the promised land all of the males were circumcised. This was a seal of the visible covenant relationship. If some Israelite couple wanted to skip this part of the initiation or got a little squeamish about cutting the foreskin from their infant boy, they would have to leave the community. If one of the non-Jews who had accompanied Israel for the last forty years had said, "I shared the desert with you, but this is too much for me," he and all his family would have been excluded from the covenant people. Visible signs were vastly important to the visible community of God. They sealed both the men and the women, the boys and the girls to the covenant promises God had made.

Yet Paul explains in Romans 2 and 1 Corinthians 3 that being part of the visible was never enough. Most Israelites had settled for the visible, without "circumcising their hearts" before God. There was no invisible, committed faith behind the outward organization for these people. As a result, "But with many of them God was not well pleased: for they were overthrown in the wilderness" (1 Corinthians 10:5). The outward realities are only meaningful if the inward realities match.

> For circumcision verily profiteth, if thou keep the law: but if thou be a breaker of the law, thy circumcision is made uncircumcision. Therefore if the uncircumcision keep the righteousness of the law, shall not his uncircumcision be counted for circumcision? And shall not uncircumcision which is by nature, if it fulfil the law, judge thee, who by the letter and circumcision dost transgress the law? For he is not a Jew, which is one outwardly; neither is that circumcision, which is outward in the flesh: But he is a Jew, which is one inwardly; and circumcision is that of the heart, in the spirit, and not in the letter. [Romans 2:25–29a]

Anyone who has read ahead in Paul's Epistle to the Romans knows where this argument is headed. No one has kept the law! So is there no invisible, true church, behind the visibly organized one? No, there is one, only because of God's grace.

The invisible church is "the whole number of elect, that have been, are, or shall be gathered together into one." The invisible church now living in the world consists of all those truly called by God and justified by faith. When this body gathers for worship, along with those who are not saved, the church becomes visible. The visible church may or may not have a building, but it has some sort of organization, human direction, and gathering point for worship, teaching, fellowship, and praise. Those of us who lead the visible church should desire to become as close as possible to the invisible church, but we will never be exactly the same as the gathering of the born-again.

This dramatically differentiates the church to which I belong from every other sort of organization with which I may affiliate. A person's name may be on a church roll. The person may be baptized and partake of the sacrament of the Lord's Supper. The person may act as a deacon, elder, preacher, or attain some other high post. But unless the person is a part of the invisible church of Christ that person is not truly a member of the Body of Christ. Only those who are truly born anew are in the only church that counts. Therefore, we had better not be satisfied with the mere externalities of religion. Religion is a matter of the heart, a transformation of the soul only the Spirit of God can bring about. All those who place their trust in Christ for salvation, and all those who abandon all trust in their own goodness and acknowledge their sinfulness, receive the blessed gift of life eternal from the pierced hands of Christ.

The imperfect body

Even the purest churches are subject to mixture and error. As the saying goes, if you ever find the perfect church, whatever you do, don't join it. You will surely mess it up. The reason for these studies is that I am convinced there is a set of teachings that corresponds closely with the truth God has revealed in Scripture. If I didn't think that, I would change what I believe until I did find such teachings. I am not so foolish as to believe, however, that I have things all figured out or that the Westminster Assembly or the reformers or the early church fathers had it all figured out. All theologians are human, and we all are sinful. Only God has the corner on truth. Still, we have undergone times in the history of the church when truth was a rare commodity, and the teaching available had degenerated until they were synagogues of Satan. One such time is now, and Christians must be wary that they part company from a congregation that refuses to submit to Scripture. That doesn't mean everyone must agree about what the Bible teaches. It does mean the Bible must be regarded as the Word of God.

A community of saints

Continuing our list of the basic teachings about the church we turn to what the *Confession* says in chapter 26, "Of the Communion of Saints." Its central point is that all of the saints of God are united to Christ and to one another by the Holy Spirit and by faith.

Sinners and saints

The word *saint* comes from the word *sanctify* and means to be cleansed or set aside to God. The *communion of the saints* does not refer to any fellowship of super-Christians that have achieved a gold medal in the Olympics of faith. The saints talked about in the Bible are not due any special adoration. They are simply we who are redeemed. The church is a *koinonia* fellowship of saints—a kind of fellowship unique to the Christian community. The Bible identifies *koinonia* as a fellowship bound into nothing less than a new race of people. Scripture recognizes many families of peoples who are loosely tied by common ancestry, culture, or skin color. The Bible teaches that these families have become alienated from one another by sin's depravity. But Scripture only recognizes the existence of two "races," and these two are the people who are God's and the people who are Satan's. All those who are God's are brothers and sisters in Christ.

As you walk into the church building's sanctuary where you hold membership, look around for a moment. Do you see brothers and sisters with whom you will spend eternity? If you are in a church where not everyone is familiar to you, get to know some of your relatives you haven't met before. Is there someone you have chosen to ignore for some reason? Be brutally honest with yourself and ask if you are turned off by some unworthy prejudice against a brother or sister—perhaps his or her clothing or background, or accent, or reputation, or skin color. You need not be best friends with every other person in the church. Those who study such things say our circle of friends in a church can exceed no more than thirty. But neither should prejudices of any sort cut us off from fellowship with the larger body. Make a special point to pray for those about whom you have negative feelings of any kind. Also, when those feelings are caused by a bitter, broken relationship, we have a special responsibility to God to be reconciled to brothers and sisters.

One of the great preachers of the past, John Jowett, wrote that the church is vastly impoverished because so little communion is exercised. We need to hear from the mature saints, those who have struggled in their own spiritual lives and who have seen victory. We need to hear how they escaped the snare, how they captured a fortified hill in their lives, how they comforted their hearts at the grave by the side of the way.

What about those who have grown old in Christ? What delicacies of insight can be shared by the aged pilgrims? Have they seen the glimmer of the golden city? Do they yearn to be with those they have loved? What can we learn from their many years? What about the young pilgrims? How are they faring? What can we do to strengthen their arms? We need to be tapped and shared in the fellowship of the saints. What are the things to be tapped and shared?

Unity in love

Every relationship should be built upon a common ground. We need to share some commonality. The Westminster framers said that our vertical fellowship with Christ communes with him "in his graces, sufferings, death, resurrection, and glory." Those are the things we hold in common with God in Jesus Christ. Think about that thought. The only things we have in common with God are those very things he has given to us. We have already likened this unity of fellowship to the relationship of a dying person rescued from the street with his loving benefactor (see pp. 86–88). The rescuer in Charles Spurgeon's story was rich and powerful; his life and experiences had nothing at all in common with those of the plague victims he saved. But out of the rescue and the victim's response there could grow a bond of fellowship.

That is the vertical fellowship with God; the horizontal fellowship is that of the shared experiences of the rescued. The *Confession* speaks of a unity of love in which believers share God's gifts and graces with one another. They also share in the common duties God has given them to do, including the duty to build one another up. Their fellowship is described as being on two levels:

1. shared experiences as inner people in whom the Spirit dwells;
2. shared experiences as outward people who live for one another's mutual good.

Intertwining lives

It is by their very profession in Christ that saints are bound to one another. *Koinonia* is not an optional but an indispensable part of Christian life in worship and mutual edification. It is the responsibility of the church that Christians also relieve each other in need, according to the abilities of the fellow believers to do so. And the *Confession* specifies that this responsibility to help one another is not solely in operation within a local family of believers. As God gives opportunity, serving fellowship extends its helping hand to "all those who, in every place, call upon the name of the Lord Jesus." Thus, evangelistic missions to neighborhoods and nations is not the church's only responsibility under the Great Commission mandate. Raising up a world witness includes enabling and encouraging believers in other places.

What communion is not

As with so many Christian doctrines, the propensity of people to extend them into areas God never intended always is a danger. The Westminster Assembly addressed two dangers related to the communion of saints that still come up occasionally today:

> This communion which the saints have with Christ, doth not make them in anywise partakers of the substance of his Godhead, or to be equal with Christ in any respect: either of which to affirm is impious and blasphemous. Nor doth their communion one with another, as saints, take away or infringe the title or property which each man hath in his goods and possessions.

Does the communion between the Christian and God make the Christian in some way akin to God himself? Some cults have said so. Mormons at the root of their theology, for example, hold to a God who is quite human-like in appetites and abilities. It is their goal to attain in afterlife to that sort of godhood, so that we (male Mormons, anyway) and God will meet and fellowship as equals. The whole point of liberal Christian theology takes another tack in tying our fellowship to a Christ who is no more God than are we. We can enjoy mystical union with this historical Jesus, and so become no more than we already are (see book 2, pp. 118–119).

The other error that often has crept into the church is that of a Christian form of communism. These idealistic communities have never achieved success for long, and at least a few of them, including the Oneida Community in the 1800s and the recent followers of David Koresh, shared even sexual intimacy with one another. One of the standard lines of the modern cult has been to force all members to renounce their families and devote themselves body and soul and finances to the fellowship. Some say that this is what the early church did in Jerusalem, which is decidedly not true. In Acts 4:36–37 Barnabas sold a field and gave it to the community treasury. He sold one field, not all that he had. In Acts 5, Ananias and Sapphira are condemned by Peter, not for withholding some of their wealth, but for lying about what they had given in order to try to gain the applause of others.

The Bible counsels to openly give of our substance for the welfare of our brothers and sisters. We are never counseled to drop out of society's economy, impoverish ourselves, and submerge ourselves in the *koinonia* of the body. *Koinonia*, like becoming one flesh in marriage, celebrates our individuality and empowers us as individual believers before God.

Other pictures of the church

The Bible uses the pictures of a body, a family, a race, and a nation or kingdom to describe *koinonia*. Other pictures also describe this fellowship.

1. We are *joint heirs* with Jesus Christ and the inheritors of all things.
2. We are the *hoi pistoi, the believers* in the living God.
3. We are *disciples or learners*, the *mathetēs*. From Christ we learn our worldview, our values, our, hope, faith, and love.
4. We are a *fellowship of slaves*. The word sometimes is translated "servant," but the meaning in Roman culture was that of a slave in bonds, the lowest level of servitude found in the Roman world. Paul delighted to call himself the "bond slave of Jesus Christ."
5. We are a *community of witnesses*. The Greek word *martys* is the origin of our word *martyr*. Originally it simply meant to proclaim one's faith, but

it came to mean to witness by giving one's life in the arena. What a oneness is created among those who put their lives on the line as they boldly witness for the living Christ. In Scripture the word *witness* can refer to a legal sense of giving testimony, to an eyewitness declaration of fact, to what is confessed, and to dying for those facts. We are witnesses in all those senses to something that is breathtakingly important to the world, the greatest event in all of history.

6. We are the *branches* and Christ is the Vine. As a fellowship we draw sustenance from our Source.
7. We are the *walking dead*. We were dead. Then we were crucified with Christ and raised with him to glory. Now we are dead to the things of the world.
8. We are *soldiers of Christ*. No one who has ever served on the front lines in war does not understand the special bonds of fellowship forged in a foxhole.

The dynamics of relationships in Christ are almost indescribable, even through these and other pictures. Nothing quite like it exists in other religions, but I have seen this mystical union around the world. I recall sitting on an airplane next to a young mother. We politely exchanged a few strained pleasantries between strangers, then got around to spiritual things. I discovered that she had accepted Christ two years before. Our conversation then unfolded easily as we found we shared an understanding about everything that mattered. We were of one mind and one heart about a world-and-life view.

We were the church.

What does the future hold in Christ?

What benefits do believers receive from Christ at death? The souls of believers are at their death made perfect in holiness, and do immediately pass into glory; and their bodies, being still united to Christ, do rest in their graves till the resurrection.

What benefits do believers receive from Christ at the resurrection? At the resurrection, believers being raised up in glory, shall be openly acknowledged and acquitted in the day of judgment, and made perfectly blessed in the full enjoying of God to all eternity. [Westminster Shorter Catechism, questions 37, 38]

7

"I Will Not Be Shaken"

As John Knox lay dying, those around the bed of the great transformer of Scotland wondered if his magnificent faith had seen him through to his end. "Hast thou hope?" they asked. Not a word did he speak in response. Knox simply lifted his finger upward and breathed his last.

As these words are written a number of Branch Davidian followers await their hope—the reincarnation of David Koresh, whose self-proclaimed messiahship went up in flames with 80 followers in the Waco, Texas, tragedy.

Here are two reactions to the problem of hope. Is either founded on a rock? I believe only one Source of hope exists today, the same Source Knox and countless others have found in their darkest hours. "Find rest, O my soul, in God alone," advises King David, the transformer of ancient Israel, "Truly my soul waiteth upon God: from him cometh my salvation. He only is my rock and my salvation; he is my defence; I shall not be greatly moved [or shaken]."

What a statement to make: In the midst of life's greatest challenges, in the midst of their own foolish sins, in the midst of impossible situations, in the midst of dying agonies, Knox and David were transformers because they were transformed people. They were transformed people because their hope was built upon the Rock of their salvation.

Living transcendently

As we conclude our tour through Scripture by way of the *Westminster Confession of Faith* and *Larger* and *Shorter* catechisms we have left some subjects untouched and exhausted none of the rich veins of truth in these documents. But we have sought a pattern for believing and living as transformed, transforming people, and now we come to the bottom line: If God is the God of the Bible, then we need only point upward to find the rest for our soul. If God has made a way of salvation in Jesus Christ and his will for our lives is good and satisfying, we have hope. If our chief end for eternity is to glorify God and to enjoy him forever, we have hope. In fact, come what may, no other people on earth have such a reason for hope.

And I saw a new heaven and a new earth: for the first heaven and the first earth were passed away; and there was no more sea. [Revelation 21:1]

To hope is to live transcendently. Hope is a confidence in something bigger than existential circumstances. This doesn't mean the person who hopes lives in a fantasy view of reality or trusts in a Koreshly confidence without foundation. The apostle Paul understood the realities quite well, yet he hoped in the Rock of salvation.

Paul saw that in the gospel is a world transforming power able to charge people with righteousness, and lack of righteousness produces hopelessness:

> For I am not ashamed of the gospel of Christ: for it is the power of God unto salvation to every one that believeth; to the Jew first, and also to the Greek. For therein is the righteousness of God revealed from faith to faith: as it is written, The just shall live by faith. [Romans 1:16–17]

He saw life's sufferings as life-transforming experiences in Christ:

> Therefore being justified by faith, we have peace with God through our Lord Jesus Christ: By whom also we have access by faith into this grace wherein we stand, and rejoice in hope of the glory of God. And not only so, but we glory in tribulations also: knowing that tribulation worketh patience; And patience, experience; and experience, hope: And hope maketh not ashamed; because the love of God is shed abroad in our hearts by the Holy Ghost which is given unto us. [Romans 5:1–5]

He saw in the world's traumas a future of transforming redemption in Christ:

> The Spirit itself beareth witness with our spirit, that we are the children of God: And if children, then heirs; heirs of God, and joint-heirs with Christ; if so be that we suffer with him, that we may be also glorified together. . . . For we know that the whole creation groaneth and travaileth in pain together until now. And not only they, but ourselves also, which have the first-fruits of the Spirit, even we ourselves groan within our-

selves, waiting for the adoption, to wit, the redemption of our body. For we are saved by hope: but hope that is seen is not hope: for what a man seeth, why doth he yet hope for? But if we hope for that we see not, then do we with patience wait for it. [Romans 8:16–17, 22–25]

In the midst of a generation that was filled with anxieties over the cold war and the nuclear sword of Damocles that hung above humanity's head, I remember sitting in a classroom at Columbia Theological Seminary listening to Dr. Manford George Gutzke, professor of Bible. He was talking about current events of the time and made a most startling statement: "They say they are going to blow up the world. Well, let them blow it up. Who needs it anyway?"

I thought, "What a bold and audacious thing for anyone to say." Gutzke believed in life that transformed situations because it pointed to a larger reality.

We live, now as when Gutzke made that statement, in a time of great fear. Two generations have grown up, married, and borne children under the threat of a thermonuclear war. That threat of global annihilation seems somewhat abated with the fall of communism, but many of the missiles are lying about in the hands of even less stable governments than that of the USSR. There are world leaders who partake in hatreds so intense that they would delight to wipe out millions of enemies with one well-placed strike. And even without nuclear capability, some of them have managed to kill hundreds, thousands, and in one African nation recently, perhaps 100,000.

Hope and fear

Hope can be hard to come by in a society that has turned away from God. A recently published study by the Annie E. Casey Foundation studied statistics in every state, finding, among other things, that in the period from 1985 to 1991 the murder rate for teenagers doubled, most killed by other teenagers. Record numbers also dropped out of school or had babies out of wedlock. The report concluded that young people in the United States, especially in the impoverished areas, live without hope for the future. Their hopelessness becomes a self-fulfilling prophecy. Without the incentive to think they can succeed, they follow their parents' track into welfare dependence, the men fathering another generation like themselves and abandoning the mothers to raise the family alone. Staggering social problems defy solutions here and around the world. There is no possibility of transforming hope unless something bigger than the problems exists.

Every generation has experienced hopelessness. For one example, in England and later in the United States during the worst abuses of the Industrial Revolution, unimaginable poverty degraded the lives of millions of people. I recall seeing a letter a wealthy German businessman received from his bank when the German mark was devalued in 1924. This man had millions of marks in the bank, but the letter informed him that they had no coins small enough to represent his account; therefore they were closing it as empty. The same thing happened in China in 1946. Certainly it could happen again. We have no basis for confidence that we will not by next week face an empty bank account in an economically devastated economy. In fact, given the level of sin in our society, it would seem only just that we should.

Then we come to Jesus, and he tells us as he did those disciples who were terrified by their circumstances and his power, "Fear not!" In the upper room as he faced the cross he told the disciples to not let their hearts be troubled—not to fear. The reason they were not to fear was not that the situation was about to improve. It most decidedly was not. The reason for their confidence was that "in my Father's house are many mansions: if it were not so, I would have told you. I go to prepare a place for you. And if I go and prepare a place for you, I will come again, and receive you unto myself; that where I am, there ye may be also" (John 14:2–3).

The *Westminster Shorter Catechism* looks at what Christ was going to prepare and summarizes it as the benefits we believers receive at death:

What benefits do believers receive from Christ at death?

The souls of believers are at their death made perfect in holiness, and do immediately pass into glory; and their bodies, being still united to Christ, do rest in their graves till the resurrection.

What a marvelous hope is thus unfolded. The apostle John, in the last two chapters of his great Revelation, pulls the curtains aside for a few moments to reveal some glimpses of those many mansions:

And I saw a new heaven and a new earth: for the first heaven and the first earth were passed away; and there was no more sea. And I John saw the holy city, new Jerusalem, coming down from God out of heaven, prepared as a bride adorned for her husband. And I heard a great voice out of heaven saying, Behold, the tabernacle of God is with men, and he will dwell with them, and they shall be his people, and God himself shall be with them, and be their God. And God shall wipe away all tears from their eyes; and there shall be no more death, neither sorrow, nor crying, neither shall there be any more pain: for the former things are passed away. [Revelation 21:1–4; compare Isaiah 65:17–25]

If the world blows up, its passing away will usher in a day without death and mourning and with God. Are such marvelous pictures as are painted by John to be taken literally or are they just symbols? In those final chapters of the Revelation John takes the most magnificent and matchless beauties known and paints with them a picture of the Holy City, New Jerusalem. If this is a mere symbolic representation of the greater reality, then it is beyond the ability of human tongue and speech to declare.

How glorious must that new heaven and new earth be. On a transparent crystalline morning, where the sunlight beams brightly and everything seems to be more alive, when there is a slight chill and yet a warmth from the sun, the wonder of the world seems impossible to surpass. How could anyone improve on such a day? And yet the finest earth day shall be as nothing, for "Eye hath not seen, nor ear heard, neither have entered into the heart of man, the things which God hath prepared for them that love him. But God hath revealed them unto us by his Spirit" (1 Corinthians 2:9–10a).

Our hope for now

In God's presence

God will create a new heaven and a new earth as the final abode of the redeemed, a new creation for his beloved. Even now he reveals it to us by his Spirit. What revelation by his Spirit? Certainly the Spirit's work in Scripture gives us some revealed information about the glories of this planned honeymoon cottage to be built by the Bridegroom for the bride. I suspect, however, that Paul here speaks of the Holy Spirit himself, for the truly great thing about our future glory is that we will be *with* God, to glorify him and to enjoy him forever. And in the Holy Spirit we now have Immanuel, "God with us" in a spiritually tangible sense. In the Holy Spirit the Christian experiences heaven. In the Spirit hope is something future we can only dimly see and not yet experience—but in the Spirit hope also is sealed to confidence we now *know*. This is the view of eternity we do not have to wait to see.

In God's glory

What else do we know about the future state of the Christian? One of the first things John tells us is that the New Jerusalem will experience the light of the glory of God, and its light will be as a transparent jasper stone. The average jasper is opaque, but there are some, about which the apostle speaks, that were clear as crystal, either blue or green. There will be no need for sun or moon, whether literally or figuratively, for the glory and brightness of God shall light it. Without night there will be no need for artificial light.

In a renewed body

How then shall we sleep? Why should we? We no longer will be in the wearying city of humanity, with its fallen, wearing-out bodies. In the city of God, why should there be weariness? Energy will never flag; enthusiasm will never dampen; a perfect body will know no limitations. There will be no more death nor sorrow nor sadness nor pain. For many, I am sure, that in itself will mean heaven. Many have not known a day without acute pain. What leaping and running for joy there will be for you who now limp along or coast in a wheelchair. No more pain in the knees, or hips, or back, or neck, or head. I think of intensely crippled Christians I have seen die, knowing that the moment their last breath was over they could turn soul somersaults like an energy-bursting, young cheerleader.

In God's renewed worship

Without the barriers between us and God of sinful bodies and guilty consciences, no steeples will dot the skyline of the Holy City. No temple or church building will be needed, for the Lamb and the Lord God Almighty are the temple. There we shall see the face of God and live—and that forever. You will not need to meditate in your heart on God. You may talk with the living Christ or the Father as a beloved, accepted spouse and child.

In God's renewed society

This new world will draw its sustaining force from God. A river of life will flow from the throne of God and the Lamb, watering the tree of life and the fruits of twelve great crops. And the tree will be for the healing of the nations. All that our hopeless society sees in the world today is sick and degraded. The world's societies seem to be represented in John's revelation of heaven, but there they will be whole and fruitful. Human society will be restored to God's original vision.

But John tells us there will be no more sea. I think that John may be saying something symbolic and significant. The "sea" in his circumstances, and in the lives of the ancients was not a place of amusement and joy. It was a place of mystery and death. Except for the bravest sailors in the most advanced nautical peoples, the Phoenicians for example, ships were never sailed beyond sight of land. There was no compass, nor charts, and the shallows were not marked. Few wished to risk their lives upon the sea.

The sea meant separation in John's life. He had been banished to the Island of Patmos and could not reach out to those he loved except by letter and prayer. Patmos is a rugged, mountainous island, and the traditional spot where John wrote is in a cave high above the coastline. From this secluded retreat one can look far out to sea, overwhelmed by aloneness and separation. He could watch the different color shadings of the waters as they broiled into angry waves with the coming of a storm. Far away lived his friends and children in the Lord. Oh, that the sea might be removed, that he might join those he loved. In the holy city Christ showed him it was clear that no longer would there be barriers—either physical or emotional. There would be no more sea.

In God's renewed identification

A marvelous directory names the residents of that city of God. Just knowing it exists gives me the same conviction it gave Paul "that neither death, nor life, nor angels, nor principalities, nor powers, nor things present, nor things to come, nor height, nor depth, nor any other creature, shall be able to separate us from the love of God, which is in Christ Jesus our Lord" (Romans 8:38–39). This directory is the Lamb's Book of Life. In it are inscribed all the names of those who have trusted in Christ, the Lamb of God who has taken away the sin of the world. God's grace is so great that that book is larger than any earthly telephone directory, for it contains the names of untold millions of people God chose to be saved before the foundation of the earth, the names of those for whom Christ died.

This is the register of the people who need not be shaken by the situations of today. We are shaken only when we have forgotten who we are. Paul wrote the victorious Epistle to the Philippians while in chains, a situation that would bring some of us to the depths. Paul surely had times of depression. Second Timothy describes a low point for the apostle. Yet even at that moment he was not shaken from his faith. In Philippians he sees his imprisonment encouraging others to speak out courageously (1:14). He knows that not all who preach have the purest of motives, but at least they are preaching the Word of God (vv. 15–18). But whatever happened, Paul said, would "turn to my salvation through your prayer, and the supply of the Spirit of Jesus Christ, according to my earnest expectation and my hope, that in nothing I shall be ashamed, but that with all boldness, as always, so now also Christ shall be magnified in my body, whether it be by life, or by death" (vv. 19–20). Notice that his hope in himself was not complete, for he hoped that he not be shaken—that he remain courageous. His hope in God was fully confident: "For to me to live is Christ, and to die is gain" (v. 21).

In his dark night of the soul, when all seemed to have left him, Paul could say with continuing confidence:

I have fought a good fight, I have finished my course, I have kept the faith: Henceforth there is laid up for me a crown of righteousness, which the Lord, the righteous judge, shall give me at that day: and not to me only, but unto all them also that love his appearing. [2 Timothy 4:7–8]

The dark side of glory

Not everyone has the ground that Paul did for his confidence. All the while we glory in the salvation of those for whom Christ died we realize that most people have good reason to be without hope in the world. Those beautiful images John saw are not for them. In fact, their lives are so cut off from God that to stand in his presence would not be beautiful at all, but condemnation itself.

While referring to the "glory of his mercy in the eternal salvation of the elect," the *Westminster Confession* considers the darker side of glory: John's vision of hopeless eternal damnation of those who are wicked and disobedient. Is this stress the result of the fact that the Westminster writers were joyless doom-sayers who missed the message of God's grace? Anyone who has followed their catalog of praise through these books knows that isn't the case. Rather, they understand that those with hope must do more than sing the song of the redeemed. That day will come, and it has now come for those men who toiled over these words so long ago. It is not yet that time for us. The fact is too clear that most of the world remains without hope and under the power of Satan. A day is coming. God has already circled it on his calendar, "when he will judge the world in righteousness by Jesus Christ." In that day the rebellious angels will be finally and irrevocably judged and cast in hell. And every man and woman who has ever lived will see the videotape of life examined with the intense scrutiny of a holy, righteous Judge. Everything we have done will be unveiled for all to see. That thought should make each of us feel a bit hopeless. The question will be whether our lives will be covered by Christ's blood. Only those who can hide under the atoning blood of Christ will be saved from joining the fate of Satan and his angels.

People say, "Well, I believe that we have our hell right here on earth." There is a certain sense in which they are right. The Bible teaches that we have a foretaste of our inheritance in this world. We get a little preview of coming attractions—the basis for hope or hopelessness. However, the foretaste of hell is only a foretaste, what Scripture describes as an "earnest" on our inheritance. When you put earnest money down on a piece of property you are promising that more will come.

The reality of the intermediate state

Two important realities must be assessed concerning the redeemed hope and contrasting unredeemed hopelessness in which people must live. First, we need to understand something of what happens at death. Second, we need to know something of the last judgment we face. Drawing together what Scripture says of the state of the person after death and the resurrection of the dead, the *Westminster Confession* presents the following propositions.

Continuing consciousness

First, at death the human body turns to dust, but the soul, which is immortal, lives on. The intermediate state is one of continued conscious existence. The Bible knows of no soul sleep, no eternal rest, no purgatory, no etherland where one has a second chance, certainly no sinking into oblivion, which is the great non-Christian hope. The dust returns to the ground it came from, says Ecclesiastes 12:7, and the spirit returns to God.

We have a partial view of this state in the transfiguration of Jesus in Matthew 17, Mark 9, and Luke 9. Peter, James, and John accompany Jesus up onto a high mountain to pray. Their prayer time, however, was interrupted by the unveiled glory of Christ and the appearance of the spirits of Elijah and Moses. These two Old Testament saints had not been sleeping. They were aware of what was going on in the plan of salvation by which they themselves would be saved. They were able to discuss, we assume with understanding, the coming passion of Christ. This must have been a particularly meaningful moment for Moses, who had not been allowed to set foot in the promised land with the children of Israel, but died and was buried by God on Mount Nebo across the Jordan River. With Elijah he now visited the land of his dreams.

Jesus gives us other indications of the high level of consciousness after death. In Luke 16 he tells a vivid story of the rich man and the beggar named Lazarus who died and lived on—Lazarus in the restoring comfort of heaven and the rich man in the torment of hell.

As Jesus hung on the cross he looked over at a fellow sufferer and promised him that *that very day* they would meet in another place. When the Romans broke the thief's legs, and he slowly suffocated from the pressure on his chest, he suddenly found himself no longer pierced through and bleeding. At that moment of joyous consciousness on the other side of the passage into death, that man found Jesus, who had gone ahead of him. That very night their spiritual bodies shared together glorious fellowship at the feasting table of God, even as Christ's body lay in a new tomb and the thief's shattered remains were heaved into the common pit grave of criminals. The thief was present as Christ appeared before the Father and laid the final perfect sacrifice for sin before him. Memories of that day's intense pain—his screams under the flogging whip, the searing spasms as the nails were driven through his wrists, and the unimaginable pain of each fight for breath—all those memories eased away, replaced by the glory of the redeemed. The day that had begun in hopelessness ended in unveiled glory.

Purpose in death

Second, as the thief learned, the soul of the righteous is received by God and stands in God's presence. For the Christian, to be absent from the body is to be at home with the Lord—death swallowed up by life. That is our purpose in death:

> For we know that if our earthly house of this tabernacle were dissolved, we have a building of God, an house not made with hands, eternal in the heavens. For in this we groan, earnestly desiring to be clothed upon with our house which is from heaven: if so be that being clothed we shall not be found naked . . . , that mortality might be swallowed up of life. Now he that hath wrought us for the selfsame thing is God, who also hath given unto us the earnest of the Spirit. [2 Corinthians 5:1–5]

Since this is the state of the situation, Paul remarks in Philippians 1:23 that he is torn between wishing to live to serve God and wishing to die to be with God. He adds that to die and be with Christ is the far superior option. The *Confession* summarizes Scripture in saying: "The souls of the righteous, being then made perfect in holiness, are received into the highest heavens, where they behold the face of God in light and glory, waiting for the full redemption of their bodies."

Third, the souls of the wicked are immediately separated from God in hell, where they also wait for the final judgment of their rebellion. The clearest indication of this again rests on Jesus' story of the rich man, a story not told as a parable, symbol, or metaphor, but to describe a time and place in historical reality. References to "sleep" in death, on the other hand, are couched in metaphor language. I believe that language mostly relates to the Bible's description of the physical body. It has been incorrectly interpreted by some to refer to the intermediate state of the soul.

Daniel 12:2 tells us that "many of them that sleep in the dust of the earth shall awake, some to everlasting life, and some to shame and everlasting contempt." Scripture invariably connects the dust of the earth with the physical body. Jude 6 describes the rebellious angels as being chained in darkness awaiting judgment. Since we know these demons still have a degree of activity in the affairs of earth, we must conclude that their darkness is the same sin-clouded consciousness of rebellion that the Bible identifies with evil. Those without Christ in the intermediate state are likely living in the same darkness that obscured Christ during their lifetime on earth.

C. S. Lewis's book *The Great Divorce* tells the fanciful story of a busload of souls from hell who go on holiday to heaven. The point Lewis makes is that, as bad as things may be in hell, those who reject God in life would act no differently in death. They would not want to live in heaven if given the choice. Their vision of God is no brighter now than it was then. Not even the rich man in Jesus' story asks to cross the great divide.

Fourth, a day is coming that will shake the world to its roots, a day when the soul and a renewed physical body will unite once again. God did not intend for us to live as disembodied souls, and at the day of resurrection that division of body and spirit will be removed. This great event will accompany the return of Christ and the final judgment of the world and its inhabitants. This area of Christian doctrine called *eschatology* is only alluded to in the *Westminster Confession* and requires a discussion far beyond the scope of this look at life in the presence of God. Worthy Christians read the Bible with far different interpretations, and I think God only intends to make four eschatological points clear in Scripture:

1. A final day of resurrection and of judgment is coming.
2. God's people should be watching for the Lord's return at all times and evangelizing the world as if the opportunity will end tonight.
3. We are to live today as if that full return has happened. We are to have the values of a fully restored kingdom of God.
4. All people will be judged in a great assize, those who are covered by the blood of Christ and those who are not.

The *Confession* says in chapter 33:

As Christ would have us to be certainly persuaded that there shall be a day of judgment, both to deter all men from sin, and for the greater consolation of the godly in their adversity: so will he have the day unknown to men, that they may shake off all carnal security and be always watchful, because they know not at what hour

the Lord will come; and may be ever prepared to say,
"Come, Lord Jesus, come quickly. Amen."

That applies to Christians as well as unbelievers. We
should all shake off carnal security so we will not be
shaken at the judgment. The standard maxim of church
work is that 20 percent of the people do 80 percent of
the work. There is an indication then, that 80 percent
of the people (plus some of the 20 percent who are
trying to accumulate points with God) have an
improper understanding of the lordship of Christ. They
will stand before Christ, and some of them will be
amazed when he says, "Go away, I don't see your name
in the Lamb's Book of Life, and I don't recognize your
face. We have never met."

Others who do know Christ but have never given him
an ounce more of their life than was required, will see
their lives blistered under the heat of his gaze. We learn
from Scripture, especially from 1 Corinthians 3, that
believers will be judged for their fruits. Their punishment for sin will be covered by the blood of Christ, but
their life's product—whether they produced the fruit
of the Spirit as submissive servants of the King—will
be lost. Paul describes our fruit as contributing materials to a building, which will one day be put to the
torch by God. Some materials won't burn; they will
stand the test: Diamonds, rubies, sapphires, and emer-
alds of love to the Master will glow with the heat of
purified sacrifice. We can't understand exactly what
those treasures will mean in the economy of heaven,
but we do know their value will be eternal and great.
We will hear those words of blessing: "Well done, good
and faithful servant."

But 1 Corinthians 3 also describes other materials
in our building—wood, hay, straw. In the intense fire
of judgment, how long will those last? Those whose

love for Christ is so listless that they plan to just get by will see all that they regarded as meaningful burned away. Says Paul, "he shall suffer loss: but he himself shall be saved; yet so as by fire."

To stand unshaken before God

It is delightful to think of all the beauties and majesty and the wonder that God has prepared for those that trust in his Son. The *Shorter Catechism* says that believers at the resurrection will be raised up in glory, found righteous before God in the day of judgment, and "made perfectly blessed in the full enjoying of God."

But my heart is filled with great heaviness that some whose names are written on the roll of the church congregation I pastor have not repented nor turned from the way of the world and the flesh and the devil. They have never embraced Jesus Christ as their own Savior and Lord. They may have taken a vow in front of a congregation in which they were solemnly asked: "Do you, in sincerity, love the Lord Jesus Christ?" They may have answered, "I do." Yet they delude themselves. Their sincere love is with the world and its pleasures. One early church father said that such people "lick the world." This world is their candy—their joy and crown. Their thoughts and energies are given to it. Their citizenship is not in heaven. Their thoughts do not dwell with Christ there. For those people, and for those who have not yet even pretended to love Christ, God has both good and grim news that comes straight from the throne room of heaven:

> I am Alpha and Omega, the beginning and the end. I will give unto him that is athirst of the fountain of the water of life freely. He that overcometh shall inherit all

things; and I will be his God, and he shall be my son. But the fearful, and unbelieving, and the abominable, and murderers, and whoremongers, and sorcerers, and idolaters, and all liars, shall have their part in the lake which burneth with fire and brimstone: which is the second death. [Revelation 21:6b–8]

The point of return or no-return

As we conclude exploring the heights and depths of what we believe about God, about salvation, and about our ultimate purpose, I pray that you have been strengthened in your understanding and your awe of the real God, *Alpha* and *Omega*, Beginning and End, Father, Son, and Holy Spirit, Creator and Redeemer. I hope you now feel the challenge to give your life to him more fully, that you know a little more of what it means to glorify God and to enjoy him forever. I also ask whether you are in fact ready to face that great day when all things will be revealed and all justice done. Have you passed days or weeks or months, or years, with more thoughts about where you will spend your two-week vacation next summer than where you will spend the next two billion trillion eons of centuries? It will either be in the paradise of God, or the pain and condign punishment of hell.

Do you know for sure that your name is written there? If you do not, then I would urge you to make sure. You do not know when that last moment of choice will come. Whenever Christ will return, the fragility of life means your point of no return may be today.

To come to Jesus Christ, to embrace him as Savior and Lord, to trust him as your Substitute who died in your place, to enthrone him as Lord and King of your soul. Those are the things that make life worth living and satisfying. They also are the foundation stones on which you can stand and not be shaken, no matter what circumstance arises.

The Westminster *pattern*

Excerpts from the *Confessions of Faith*, the *Shorter Catechism*, and the *Larger Catechism*.

Transforming Truths

I t is no compliment to be called a "puritan." The epithet depicts a dour prude, without joy or a living faith. That is just about as inaccurate a description of the historic Puritans as can be imagined. In fact, Sir Thomas More, an opponent of the Puritans in England, charged that the Protestant was one who was "dronke of the new must [wine] of lewd lightnes of minde and vayne gladnesse of harte."

Such a description might well apply to one who has been transformed by God and is being continually conformed to God's will by the presence of the Holy Spirit within. Each of us is transformed more and more as we learn to glorify God and to enjoy him forever. If that is "lewd lightnes of minde and vayne gladnesse of harte," then our world and our churches need it. Whatever you think of being a puritan, I hope these books drawing on the Puritan *Westminster Confession of Faith* and the *Larger* and *Shorter* catechisms have lightened and enlightened your mind about the glory of God, the thrill of his mercy in Christ, and the satisfying life found in following his perfect will. Such gladness of heart is hardly vain.

Since these documents are not commonly familiar, and they are well worth reading in total, it seems appropriate to collect at least excerpts as a reference. Space does not permit extensive quotations from the *Confession of Faith* itself, so I include only snippets from its chapters. Most of the selections that follow are from the catechisms, in general following the sequence of the *Shorter Catechism*, since its answers offer the most precise and easy-to-remember explanations of Christian doctrine I have ever heard. In fact, we have two groups of questions and answers because the Westminster framers intended the *Shorter Catechism* to be memorized by children and the *Larger Catechism* by adults. That is embarrassing to some of us who pride ourselves on knowing the children's answers. We ministers will be especially chagrined. The Westminster divines believed ministers should memorize both sets, and commit to mind the *Confession* as well.

Wherefore seeing we also are compassed about with so great a cloud of witnesses, let us lay aside every weight, and the sin which doth so easily beset us, and let us run with patience the race that is set before us, looking unto Jesus the author and finisher of our faith; who for the joy that was set before him endured the cross, despising the shame, and is set down at the right hand of the throne of God. [Hebrews 12:1–2]

While memorizing some of these answers should not take the place of learning Scripture, I suggest that you will enrich your mind if you know, or at least become familiar with, the questions and answers that follow. Most are taken from the first half of the two documents, covering what we should believe concerning God. The section on the Ten Commandments is from the second half of the *Shorter Catechism*, concerning the duty God requires of us.

The headings refer to the "quest questions" used throughout these chapters.

Who am I?

Shorter Catechism 1. What is the chief end of man? Man's chief end is to glorify God, and to enjoy him forever.

How can I know any ultimate truth for certain?

S. C. 2. What rule hath God given to direct us how we may glorify and enjoy him? The word of God, which is contained in the Scriptures of the Old and New Testaments, is the only rule to direct us how we may glorify and enjoy him.

Larger Catechism 4. How doth it appear that the Scriptures are the word of God? The Scriptures manifest themselves to be the word of God, by their majesty and purity; by the consent of all the parts, and the scope of the whole, which is to give all glory to God; by their light and power to convince and convert sinners, to comfort and build up believers unto salvation: but the Spirit of God bearing witness by and with the Scriptures in the heart of man, is alone able fully to persuade it that they are the very word of God.

S. C. 3. What do the Scriptures principally teach? The Scriptures principally teach what man is to believe concerning God, and what duty God requires of man.

Confession, chapter 1. The authority of the holy Scripture, for which it ought to be believed and obeyed, dependeth not upon the testimony of any man or church, but wholly upon God (who is truth itself), the Author thereof; and therefore it is to be received because it is the word of God. . . . The whole counsel of God, concerning all things necessary for his own glory, man's salvation, faith, and life, is either expressly set down in Scripture, or by good and necessary consequence may be deduced from Scripture. . . . All things in Scripture are not alike plain in themselves, nor alike clear unto all; yet those things which are necessary to be known, believed, and observed, for salvation, are so clearly propounded and opened in some place of Scripture or other, that not only the learned, but the unlearned, in a due use of the ordinary means, may attain unto a sufficient understanding of them.

Is there a Source of ultimate truth?

L. C. 2. How doth it appear that there is a God? The very light of nature in man, and the works of God, declare plainly that there is a God; but his word and Spirit only do sufficiently and effectually reveal him unto men for their salvation.

Who or What is the Source of ultimate truth?

S. C. 4. What is God? God is a Spirit, infinite, eternal, and unchangeable, in his being, wisdom, power, holiness, justice, goodness, and truth.

S. C. 5. Are there more Gods than one? There is but One only, the living and true God.

S. C. 6. How many persons are there in the Godhead? There are three persons in the Godhead; the Father, the Son, and the Holy Ghost; and these three are one God, the same in substance, equal in power and glory.

L. C. 10. What are the personal properties of the three persons in the Godhead? It is proper to the Father to beget the Son, and to the Son to be begotten of the Father, and to the Holy Ghost to proceed from the Father and the Son from all eternity.

L. C. 11. How doth it appear that the Son and the Holy Ghost are God equal with the Father? The Scriptures manifest that the Son and the Holy Ghost are God equal with the Father, ascribing unto them such names, attributes, works, and worship, as are proper to God only.

Is anyone in control out there?

S. C. 7. What are the decrees of God? The decrees of God are, his eternal purpose, according to the counsel of his will, whereby, for his own glory, he hath foreordained whatsoever comes to pass.

L. C. 18. What are God's works of providence? God's works of providence are his most holy, wise, and powerful preserving and governing all his creatures; ordering them, and all their actions, to his own glory.

S. C. 8. How doth God execute his decrees? God executeth his decrees in the works of creation and providence.

S. C. 9. What is the work of creation? The work of creation is, God's making all things of nothing, by the word of his power, in the space of six days, and all very good.

S. C. 10. How did God create man? God created man male and female, after his own image, in knowledge, righteousness, and holiness, with dominion over the creatures.

S. C. 11. What are God's works of providence? God's works of providence are, his most holy, wise, and powerful preserving and governing all his creatures and all their actions.

S. C. 12. What special act of providence did God exercise towards man in the estate wherein he was created? When God had created man, he entered into a covenant of life with him, upon condition of perfect obedience; forbidding him to eat of the tree of the knowledge of good and evil, upon the pain of death.

Confession, chapter 5. The almighty power, unsearchable wisdom, and infinite goodness of God so far manifest themselves in his providence that it extendeth itself even to the first fall, and all other sins of angels and men, and that not by a bare permission, but such as hath joined with it a most wise and powerful bounding, and otherwise ordering and governing of them, in a manifold dispensation, to his only holy ends; yet so as the sinfulness thereof proceedeth only from the creature, and not from God; who, being most holy and righteous, neither is nor can be the author or approver of sin.

If there is a good God, why . . . ?

S. C. 13. Did our first parents continue in the estate wherein they were created? Our first parents, being left to the freedom of their own will, fell from the estate wherein they were created, by sinning against God.

S. C. 14. What is sin? Sin is any want of conformity unto, or transgression of, the law of God.

S. C. 15. What was the sin whereby our first parents fell from the estate wherein they were created? The sin whereby our first parents fell from the estate wherein they were created, was their eating the forbidden fruit.

S. C. 16. Did all mankind fall in Adam's first transgression? The covenant being made with Adam, not only for himself, but for his posterity; all mankind, descending from him by ordinary generation, sinned in him, and fell with him, in his first transgression.

S. C. 17. Into what estate did the fall bring mankind? The fall brought mankind into an estate of sin and misery.

S. C. 18. Wherein consists the sinfulness of that estate whereinto man fell? The sinfulness of that estate whereinto man fell, consists in the guilt of Adam's first sin, the want of original righteousness, and the corruption of his whole nature, which is commonly called Original Sin; together with all actual transgressions which proceed from it.

S. C. 19. What is the misery of that estate whereinto man fell? All mankind by their fall lost communion with God, are under his wrath and curse, and so made liable to all miseries in this life, to death itself, and to the pains of hell forever.

L. C. 27. What misery did the fall bring upon mankind? The fall brought upon mankind the loss of communion with God, his displeasure and curse; so as we are by nature children of wrath, bond slaves to Satan, and justly liable to all punishments in this world, and that which is to come.

L. C. 28. What are the punishments of sin in this world? The punishments of sin in this world are either inward, as blindness of mind, a reprobate sense, strong delusions, hardness of heart, horror of conscience, and vile affections; or outward, as the curse of God upon the creatures for our sakes, and all other evils that befall us in our bodies, names, estates, relations, and employments, together with death itself.

L. C. 29. What are the punishments of sin in the world to come? The punishments of sin in the world to come, are everlasting separation from the comfortable presence of God, and most grievous torments in soul and body, without intermission, in hell-fire forever.

S. C. 20. Did God leave all mankind to perish in the estate of sin and misery? God having, out of his mere good pleasure, from all eternity, elected some to everlasting life, did enter into a covenant of grace to deliver them out of the estate of sin and misery, and to bring them into an estate of salvation by a Redeemer.

How did Jesus Christ make a way to God?

L. C. 31. With whom was the covenant of grace made? The covenant of grace was made with Christ as the second Adam, and in him with all the elect as his seed.

L. C. 32. How is the grace of God manifested in the second covenant [of grace]? The grace of God is manifested in the second covenant, in that he freely provideth and offereth to sinners a Mediator, and life and salvation by him; and requiring faith as the condition to interest them in him, promiseth and giveth his Holy Spirit to all his elect, to work in them that faith, with all other saving graces, and to enable them unto all holy obedience, as the evidence of the truth of their faith and thankfulness to God, and as the way which he hath appointed them to salvation.

L. C. 34. How was the covenant of grace administered under the Old Testament? The covenant of grace was administered under the Old Testament, by promises, prophecies, sacrifices, circumcision, the Passover, and other types and ordinances, which did all fore-signify Christ then to come, and were for that time sufficient to build up the elect in faith in the promised Messiah, by whom they then had full remission of sin, and eternal salvation.

L. C. 35. How is the covenant of grace administered under the New Testament? Under the New Testament, when Christ the substance was exhibited, the same covenant of grace was and still is to be administered in the preaching of the word, and the administration of the sacraments of baptism and the Lord's supper; in which grace and salvation are held forth in more fulness, evidence, and efficacy, to all nations.

S. C. 21. Who is the Redeemer of God's elect? The only Redeemer of God's elect is the Lord Jesus Christ, who, being the eternal Son of God, became man, and so was, and continueth to be, God and man in two distinct natures, and one person, forever.

L. C. 38. Why was it requisite that the Mediator should be God? It was requisite that the Mediator should be God, that he might sustain and keep the human nature from sinking under the infinite wrath of God, and the power of death,

give worth and efficacy to his sufferings, obedience, and intercession; and to satisfy God's justice, procure his favor, purchase a peculiar people, give his Spirit to them, conquer all their
enemies, and bring them to everlasting salvation.

L. C. 39. Why was it requisite that the Mediator should
be man? It was requisite that the Mediator should
be man, that he might advance our nature, perform obedience to the law, suffer and make intercession for us in our nature, have a fellow-feel-
ing of our infirmities; that we might receive the
adoption of sons, and have comfort and access
with boldness unto the throne of grace.

L. C. 40. Why was it requisite that the Mediator should
be God and man in one person? It was requisite
that the Mediator, who was to reconcile God and
man, should himself be both God and man, and
this in one person, that the proper works of each
nature might be accepted of God for us, and relied
on by us, as the works of the whole person.

S. C. 22. How did Christ, being the Son of God, become
man? Christ, the Son of God, became man, by taking to himself a true body, and a reasonable soul,
being conceived by the power of the Holy Ghost,
in the womb of the Virgin Mary, and born of her,
yet without sin.

S. C. 23. What offices doth Christ execute as our
Redeemer? Christ as our Redeemer, executeth the
offices of a prophet, of a priest, and of a king, both
in his estate of humiliation and exaltation.

S. C. 24. How doth Christ execute the office of a
prophet? Christ executeth the office of a prophet,
in revealing to us, by his word and Spirit, the will
of God for our salvation.

S. C. 25. How doth Christ execute the office of a priest? Christ executeth the office of a priest, in his once offering up of himself a sacrifice to satisfy divine justice, and reconcile us to God, and in making continual intercession for us.

S. C. 26. How doth Christ execute the office of a king? Christ executeth the office of a king, in subduing us to himself, in ruling and defending us, and in restraining and conquering all his and our enemies.

S. C. 27. Wherein did Christ's humiliation consist? Christ's humiliation consisted in his being born, and that in a low condition, made under the law, undergoing the miseries of this life, the wrath of God, and the cursed death of the cross; in being buried, and continuing under the power of death for a time.

S. C. 28. Wherein consisteth Christ's exaltation? Christ's exaltation consisteth in his rising again from the dead on the third day, in ascending up into heaven, in sitting at the right hand of God the Father, and in coming to judge the world at the last day.

How can someone come to Christ?

S. C. 29. How are we made partakers of the redemption purchased by Christ? We are made partakers of the redemption purchased by Christ, by the effectual application of it to us by his Holy Spirit.

S. C. 30. How doth the Spirit apply to us the redemption purchased by Christ? The Spirit applieth to us the redemption purchased by Christ, by working faith in us, and thereby uniting us to Christ in our effectual calling.

L. C. 66. What is that union which the elect have with Christ? The union which the elect have with Christ is the work of God's grace, whereby they are spiritually and mystically, yet really and inseparably, joined to Christ as their head and husband; which is done in their effectual calling.

S. C. 31. What is effectual calling? Effectual calling is the work of God's Spirit, whereby, convincing us of our sin and misery, enlightening our minds in the knowledge of Christ, and renewing our wills, he doth persuade and enable us to embrace Jesus Christ, freely offered to us in the gospel.

Confession, chapter 7. Man by his fall having made himself incapable of life by that covenant, the Lord was pleased to make a second, commonly called the covenant of grace: wherein he freely offered unto sinners life and salvation by Jesus Christ, requiring of them faith in him that they may be saved, and promising to give unto all those that are ordained unto life his Holy Spirit, to make them willing and able to believe. . . . Under the gospel, when Christ the substance was exhibited, the ordinances in which this covenant is dispensed are the preaching of the word and the administration of the sacraments of Baptism and the Lord's Supper; which, though fewer in number, and administered with more simplicity and less outward glory [than the Old Testament sacrifices and rituals], yet in them is held forth in more fullness, evidence, and spiritual efficacy, to all nations, both Jews and Gentiles; and is called the New Testament. There are not, therefore, two covenants of grace differing in substance, but one and the same under various dispensations. [In other words, both Old Testament and New Testament believers must be saved in the same way—through justification by faith in the atoning death of Christ. See also chapter 11: "The justification of believers under the Old Testament was, in all these respects, one and the same with the justification of believers under the New Testament."]

What do we do about guilt?

S. C. 32. What benefits do they that are effectually called partake of in this life? They that are effectually called do in this life partake of justification, adoption, and sanctification, and the several benefits which in this life do either accompany or flow from them.

S. C. 33. What is justification? Justification is an act of God's free grace, wherein he pardoneth all our sins, and accepteth us as righteous in his sight, only for the righteousness of Christ imputed to us, and received by faith alone.

What does it mean that Christians are adopted?

S. C. 34. What is adoption? Adoption is an act of God's free grace, whereby we are received into the number, and have a right to all the privileges of the sons of God.

Confession, chapter 12. All those that are justified God vouchsafeth, in and for his only Son Jesus Christ, to make partakers of the grace of adoption; by which they are taken into the number, and enjoy the liberties and privileges of the children of God; have his name put upon them; receive the Spirit of adoption; have access to the throne of grace with boldness; are enabled to cry *Abba*, Father; are pitied, protected, provided for, and chastened by him as by a father; yet never cast off, but sealed to the day of redemption, and inherit the promises, as heirs of everlasting salvation.

What is a sanctified life?

S. C. 35. What is sanctification? Sanctification is the work of God's free grace, whereby we are renewed in the whole man after the image of God, and are enabled more and more to die unto sin, and live unto righteousness.

S. C. 36. What are the benefits which in this life do accompany or flow from justification, adoption, and sanctification? The benefits which in this life do accompany or flow from justification, adoption, and sanctification, are, assurance of God's love, peace of conscience, joy in the Holy Ghost, increase of grace, and perseverance therein to the end.

Confession, chapter 16. Good works are only such as God hath commanded in his holy Word, and no such as, without the warrant thereof, are devised by men out of blind zeal, or upon any pretense of good intention. These good works, done in obedience to God's commandments, are the fruits and evidences of a true and lively faith; and by them believers manifest their thankfulness, strengthen their assurance, edify their brethren, adorn the profession of the gospel, stop the mouths of the adversaries, and glorify God, whose workmanship they are, created in Christ Jesus thereunto, that, having their fruit unto holiness, they may have the end, eternal life.

What is saving faith?

S. C. 86. What is faith in Jesus Christ? Faith in Jesus Christ is a saving grace, whereby we receive and rest upon him alone for salvation, as he is offered to us in the gospel.

Confession, chapter 14. The grace of faith, whereby the elect are enabled to believe to the saving of their souls, is the work of the Spirit of Christ in their hearts, and is ordinarily wrought by the ministry of the Word; by which also, and by the administration of the sacraments and prayer, it is increased and strengthened. By this faith a Christian believeth to be true whatsoever is revealed in the Word, for the authority of God himself speaking therein; and acteth differently upon that which each particular passage thereof containeth; yielding obedience to the commands, trembling at the threatenings, and embracing the promises of God for this life and that which is to come. But the principal acts of saving faith are accepting, receiving, and resting upon Christ alone for justification, sanctification, and eternal life, by virtue of the covenant of grace.

What does it mean to repent?

S. C. 87. What is repentance unto life? Repentance unto life is a saving grace, whereby a sinner, out of a true sense of his sin, and apprehension of the mercy of God in Christ, doth, with grief and hatred of his sin, turn from it unto God, with full purpose of, and endeavor after, new obedience.

Confession, chapter 15. Although repentance be not to be rested in as any satisfaction for sin, or any cause of the pardon thereof, which is the act of God's free grace in Christ; yet is it of such necessity to all sinners that none may expect pardon without it. As there is no sin so small but it deserves damnation, so there is no sin so great that it can bring damnation upon those who truly repent. Men ought not to content themselves with a general repentance, but it is every man's duty to endeavor to repent of his particular sins particularly. As every man is bound to make private confession of his sins to God, praying for the pardon thereof, upon which, and the forsaking of them, he shall find mercy; so he that scandalizeth his brother, or the Church of Christ, ought to be willing, by a private or public confession and sorrow for his sin, to declare his repentance to those that are offended, who are thereupon to be reconciled to him, and in love to receive him.

What assurances does the Christian have in death?

L. C. 85. Death, being the wages of sin, why are not the righteous delivered from death, seeing all their sins are forgiven in Christ? The righteous shall be delivered from death itself at the last day, and even in death are delivered from the sting and curse of it; so that, although they die, yet it is out of God's love, to free them perfectly from sin and misery, and to make them capable of further communion with Christ, in glory, which they then enter upon.

S. C. 37. What benefits do believers receive from Christ at death? The souls of believers are at their death made perfect in holiness, and do immediately pass into glory; and their bodies, being still united to Christ, do rest in their graves, till the resurrection.

L. C. 79. May not true believers, by reason of their imperfections, and the many temptations and sins they are overtaken with, fall away from the state of grace? True believers, by reason of the unchangeable love of God, and his decree and covenant to give them perseverance, their inseparable union with Christ, his continual intercession for them, and the Spirit and seed of God abiding in them, can neither totally nor finally fall away from the state of grace, but are kept by the power of God through faith unto salvation.

L. C. 81. Are all true believers at all times assured of their present being in the estate of grace, and that they shall be saved? Assurance of grace and salvation not being of the essence of faith, true believers may wait long before they obtain it; and, after the enjoyment thereof, may have it weakened and intermitted, through manifold distempers, sins, temptations, and desertions; yet are they never left without such a presence and support of the Spirit of God as keeps them from sinking into utter despair.

Confession, chapter 17. They whom God accepteth in his Beloved, effectually called and sanctified by his Spirit, can neither totally nor finally fall away from the state of grace; but shall certainly persevere therein to the end. . . . Nevertheless they may, through the temptations of Satan and of the world, the prevalency of corruption remaining in them, and the neglect of the means of their preservation, fall into grievous sins; and for a time continue therein; whereby they incur God's displeasure, and grieve his Holy Spirit; come to be deprived of some measure of their graces and comforts; have their hearts hardened, and their consciences wounded; hurt and scandalize others, and bring temporal judgments upon themselves.

What makes an ethical standard "Christian"?

S. C. 42. What is the sum of the ten commandments? The sum of the ten commandments is, To love the

Lord our God with all our heart, with all our soul, with all our strength, and with all our mind; and our neighbor as ourselves.

S. C. 46. What is required in the first commandment? The first commandment requireth us to know and acknowledge God to be the only true God, and our God; and to worship and glorify him accordingly.

S. C. 47. What is forbidden in the first commandment? The first commandment forbiddeth the denying, or not worshiping and glorifying the true God as God, and our God, and the giving of that worship and glory to any other, which is due to him alone.

S. C. 50. What is required in the second commandment? The second commandment requireth the receiving, observing, and keeping pure and entire, all such religious worship and ordinances as God hath appointed in his word.

S. C. 51. What is forbidden in the second commandment? The second commandment forbiddeth the worshiping of God by images, or any other way not appointed in his word.

S. C. 54. What is required in the third commandment? The third commandment requireth the holy and reverend use of God's names, titles, attributes, ordinances, word, and works.

S. C. 55. What is forbidden in the third commandment? The third commandment forbiddeth all profaning or abusing of anything whereby God maketh himself known.

S. C. 58. What is required in the fourth commandment? The fourth commandment requireth the keeping holy to God such set times as he hath appointed in his word; expressly one whole day in seven, to be a holy sabbath to himself.

S. C. 61. What is forbidden in the fourth commandment? The fourth commandment forbiddeth the omission or careless performance of the duties required, and the profaning the day by idleness, or doing that which is in itself sinful, or by unnecessary thoughts, words, or works, about our worldly employments or recreations.

S. C. 64. What is required in the fifth commandment? The fifth commandment requireth the preserving the honor, and performing the duties, belonging to everyone in their several places and relations, as superiors, inferiors, or equals.

S. C. 65. What is forbidden in the fifth commandment? The fifth commandment forbiddeth the neglecting of, or doing anything against, the honor and duty which belongeth to everyone in their several places and relations.

S. C. 68. What is required in the sixth commandment? The sixth commandment requireth all lawful endeavors to preserve our own life, and the life of others.

S. C. 69. What is forbidden in the sixth commandment? The sixth commandment forbiddeth the taking away of our own life, or the life of our neighbor unjustly, or whatsoever tendeth thereunto.

S. C. 71. What is required in the seventh commandment? The seventh commandment requireth the preservation of our own and our neighbor's chastity, in heart, speech, and behavior.

S. C. 72. What is forbidden in the seventh commandment? The seventh commandment forbiddeth all unchaste thoughts, words, and actions.

S. C. 74. What is required in the eighth commandment? The eighth commandment requireth the lawful procuring and furthering the wealth and outward estate of ourselves and others.

S. C. 75. What is forbidden in the eighth commandment? The eighth commandment forbiddeth whatsoever doth or may unjustly hinder our own or our neighbor's wealth or outward estate.

S. C. 77. What is required in the ninth commandment? The ninth commandment requireth the maintaining and promoting of truth between man and man, and of our own and our neighbor's good name, especially in witness-bearing.

S. C. 78. What is forbidden in the ninth commandment? The ninth commandment forbiddeth whatsoever is prejudicial to truth, or injurious to our own or our neighbor's good name.

S. C. 80. What is required in the tenth commandment? The tenth commandment requireth full contentment with our own condition, with a right and charitable frame of spirit toward our neighbor, and all that is his.

S. C. 81. What is forbidden in the tenth commandment? The tenth commandment forbiddeth all discontentment with our own estate, envying or grieving at the good of our neighbor, and all inordinate motions and affections to anything that is his.

S. C. 82. Is any man able perfectly to keep the commandments of God? No mere man since the fall is able in this life perfectly to keep the commandments of God, but doth break them in thought, word, and deed.

S. C. 85. What doth God require of us, that we may escape his wrath and curse due to us for sin? To escape the wrath and curse of God due to us for sin, God requireth of us faith in Jesus Christ, repentance unto life, with the diligent use of all the outward means whereby Christ communicateth to us the benefits of redemption.

How is life made free in Christ?

Confession, chapter 20. The liberty which Christ hath purchased for believers under the gospel consists in their freedom from the guilt of sin, the condemning wrath of God, the curse of the moral law; and in their being delivered from this present evil world, bondage to Satan, and dominion of sin, from the evil of afflictions, the sting of death, the victory of the grave, and everlasting damnation; as also in their free access to God, and their yielding obedience unto him, not out of slavish fear, but a child-like love and a willing mind. . . . God alone is Lord of the conscience, and hath left it free from the doctrines and commandments of men which are in any thing contrary to his Word, or beside it in matters of faith or worship. . . . They who, upon pretense of Christian liberty, do practice any sin, or cherish any lust, do thereby destroy the end of Christian liberty; which is, that, being delivered out of the hands of our enemies, we might serve the Lord without fear, in holiness and righteousness before him, all the days of our life.

How is life made rich in Christ?

Confession, chapter 21. The light of nature showeth that there is a God, who hath lordship and sovereignty over all; is good, and doeth good unto all; and is therefore to be feared, loved, praised, called upon, trusted in, and served with all the heart, and with all the soul, and with all the might. But the acceptable way of worshiping the true God is instituted by himself, and so limited by his own revealed will, that he may not be worshiped according to the imaginations and devices of men, or the suggestions of Satan, under any visible representation or any other way not prescribed in the Holy Scripture. . . . This Sabbath is then kept holy unto the Lord, when men, after a due preparing of their hearts, and ordering of their common affairs beforehand, do not only observe an holy rest all the day from their own works, words, and thoughts, about their worldly employments and recreations; but also are taken up the whole time in the public and private exercises of his worship, and in the duties of necessity and mercy.

What makes relationships whole in Christ?

L. C. 62. What is the visible church? The visible church is a society made up of all such as in all ages and places of the world do profess the true religion, and of their children.

L. C. 64. What is the invisible church? The invisible church is the whole number of the elect that have been, are, or shall be gathered into one under Christ the head.

Confession, chapter 24. Marriage was ordained for the mutual help of husband and wife; for the increase of mankind with a legitimate issue, and of the Church with an holy seed; and for preventing of uncleanness. . . . Although the corruption of man be such as is apt to study arguments, unduly to put asunder those whom God hath joined together in marriage; yet nothing but adultery, or such wilful desertion as can no way be remedied by the Church or civil magistrate, is cause sufficient.

Confession, chapter 25. The catholic or universal Church, which is invisible, consists of the whole number of the elect, that have been, are, or shall be gathered into one, under Christ the head thereof; and is the spouse, the body, the fulness of him that filleth all in all.

Confession, chapter 26. All saints that are united to Jesus Christ their head, by his Spirit and by faith, have fellowship with him in his graces, sufferings, death, resurrection, and glory: and being united to one another in love, they have communion in each other's gifts and graces, and are obliged to the performance of such duties, public and private, as do conduce to their mutual good, both in the inward and outward man.

What does the future hold in Christ?

L. C. 86. What is the communion in glory with Christ, which the members of the invisible church enjoy immediately after death? The communion in glory with Christ, which the members of the invisible church enjoy immediately after death, is, in that their souls are then made perfect in holiness, and received into the highest heavens, where they behold the face of God in light and glory, waiting for the full redemption of their bodies, which even in death continue united to Christ, and rest in their graves as in their beds, till at the return of Christ they be again united to their souls. Whereas the souls of the wicked are at their death cast into hell, where they remain in torments and utter darkness, and their bodies kept in their graves, as in their prisons, till the resurrection and judgment of the great day.

L. C. 87. What are we to believe concerning the resurrection? We are to believe, that at the last time there shall be a resurrection of the dead, both of the just and unjust; when they that are then found alive shall in a moment be changed; and the self-same bodies of the dead which were laid in the grave, being then again united to their souls forever, shall be raised up by the power of Christ. The bodies of the just, by the Spirit of Christ, and by virtue of his resurrection as their head, shall be raised in power, spiritual, incorruptible, and made like to his glorious body; and the bodies of the wicked shall be raised up in dishonor by him, as an offended judge.

L. C. 88. What shall follow after the resurrection? After the resurrection of the just and the unjust shall follow the final judgment of angels and men. That all may watch and pray and be ready for the coming of the Lord, the day and hour whereof no man knoweth.

S. C. 38. What benefits do believers receive from Christ at the resurrection? At the resurrection, believers being raised up in glory, shall be openly acknowledged and acquitted in the day of judgment, and made perfectly blessed in the full enjoying of God to all eternity.

Study Guide

Introduction

Words to define

God's will
vanity

idolatry
ethics

Points to ponder

1. To live a victorious life we must believe that God is good and that his will for our lives is excellent.

2. All other ways besides God's way end in meaninglessness.

Questions to answer

1. Why do we fear to put our lives in submission to God's will? Is there a part of us that wants to believe Satan's lie that God is out to get us?

2. What did the preacher mean by the term "egola-try"? In what ways does society practice this form of idol worship? Does the church also fall prey to it? Why does the preacher worry that we might not survive this way of thinking?

3. When Jesus said, "Not my will but thine be done," he knew God's will perfectly, and he knew its cost. How can we follow God's will when we don't know what it is and what it will cost?

4. What is Jeremiah looking for when he seeks the ancient ways? Is he telling us to leave modern civilization and try to re-create an ancient, more honorable and holy way of life? How can we take ancient ways and live them for the twenty-first century?

5. What does Micah 6:6–8 tell us about God's will for us? Do these principles apply to any area of behavior and values?

6. Among the kinds of people described by Solomon, which kind seems most admirable? Which seems most selfish? Why does Solomon describe them all as a chasing after wind? What is he looking for in value? Where does he finally find it?

Notebook

Through books 1 and 2 of this series you have been asked to keep a notebook to answer questions and to help you think through and personally apply the issues raised. In book 3 your notes should focus on what it means to live in such a way that you glorify God and begin to enjoy him forever. A place to start might be the negative list in 2 Timothy 3:1–5. If each of those attributes of worldly society is the antipathy of God glorifying ethics, write a corresponding list of traits God wants to see in his own society.

Chapter 1: The Cut-Flower Generation

Words to define

absolute ethics   speculative ethics   pragmatism
summum bonum utilitarianism   egoism
situation ethics   statistical ethics   altruism
existentialism   teleological ethics

Points to ponder

1. Christians can glorify and enjoy God because they are made new, their ethical system works, and they have God's presence.

2. The law reveals the will of God and binds the Christian to obey out of faith expressing itself through love.

3. The only possible way to consistently follow Jesus Christ and live according to the Christian ethic is by the power of the Spirit of God.

Questions to answer

1. How does the fact that Christians are free from the penalty of God's law empower them to keep the law? Does God's law still have relevance in the Christian life, since salvation is by grace?

2. What are the basic purposes underlying any ethical system? What should the system do for the individual? For human relationships? For relationships between the individual person and God?

3. What is meant by "speculative" ethics? If a speculative ethical system such as situation ethics is built on love for others, why can't it be considered as Christian?

4. Do Christian ethics have fundamentally different purposes and foundational principles than other ethical systems? What distinguishes those principles from every other system? Is it true that no other system can truly work?

5. What two-fold standard is at the core of Christian ethics? How does it provide a foundation for keeping the Ten Commandments?

6. What does Elton Trueblood mean by calling late twentieth-century humanity the "cut-flower generation"?

7. How does being filled with the Holy Spirit provide freedom in the ethical decisions of life? How does it provide joy?

Notebook

The application of an ethical system to specific cases is called *casuistry.* In this chapter we argued that the Christian ethical system is built upon absolute principles revealing God's will. We still must pray for wisdom in discerning how to behave in some difficult circumstances. Look for biblical help in determining whether taking a life would be murder in God's sight if: the person is threatening the life of another with a weapon; the person is verbally threatening to kill someone; the person has committed murder; the person is an abortionist; the person is in severe chronic pain; the person is an enemy soldier in wartime. If any of these, or other, situations justifies taking a life, does that mean Christians lack an absolute ethical system?

Chapter 2: Good Advice and Good News

Words to define

lawlessness	theocracy	family law
antinomians	ceremonial law	social law
theonomy	criminal law	civil law

Points to ponder

1. The law *directs* and, in a different sense than for the one outside of Christ, *binds* the child of God to loving obedience.

2. The basic message of Christianity is not *do* but *done*. Christians are not saved because they do what the law says. They are saved because the law-keeping was done by Christ.

3. The law is important to the non-Christian because it reveals sin, reveals the awfulness of sin, stirs up sin, and shows that the only hope of the sinful heart is Jesus Christ.

Questions to answer

1. Other nations had legal systems before the Ten Commandments were given on Mount Sinai. What was it about this code of laws that set apart Israel from all other nations? Why might God have given the commandments with such terrifying directness?

2. If Norman Lear is right that solutions to our problems as a society lie beyond the reach of politics to solve, can politics and government play any part in those solutions? What about Lear's own entertainment industry?

3. In what ways does the principle of the extended, open hand change civil law as it is usually practiced today?

4. This chapter applies criminal law to the problems of impurity and immorality in the church. Why is loving discipline so rarely practiced in the church today? If the principle of an eye for an eye were justly practiced in the criminal courts today, how might our justice system be different?

5. The three principles of family law—mutual respect, a chain of authority, and protection by the community—obviously are not working well today. If you are married, what can you do to strengthen your own family in these areas? What responsibility does the church have in family law?

6. What is missing from the federal and state/province social care system now in place? Is it an exaggeration to say that the Hebrew slavery system was more loving and helpful in breaking the cycle of poverty?

7. In what way are we still under the law's ceremonial system? How should this thought direct our worship?

Notebook

Meditate on the two tables of the law of God, the first four directing our duty to God, the last six our duty to other people. Direct your thinking to some aspect of God's character or will that is illustrated by each commandment. Again thinking about each law in turn, what benefit does each provide for us as God's creatures? Some Christian ethicists have said that in order to break any of the first nine laws one must first break the tenth commandment against coveting. What would be coveted in breaking each law?

Chapter 3: "Give Me Liberty!"

Words to define

freedom of conscience   pietism
civil liberty   wall of separation
spiritual liberty   Judeo-Christian ethic

Points to ponder

1. The true attitude of Christian liberty is an attitude of controlled, disciplined defiance in the face of force—the spiritual powers that would enslave us to sin again.

2. We are freed from the bondage of sin to live without guilt in Christ's presence. This is an invitation to self-discipline and service to others.

3. Only when we hold a high view of God and his Word will we understand Christian liberty and so be able to uphold non-negotiable values before society.

Questions to answer

1. What do the freedoms mentioned in the *Westminster Confession* have to say about the care with which we live for Christ?

2. What makes an issue non-negotiable to the Christian? Can you think of an example of a tenet of faith or action that should be non-negotiable to the Christian and the body of Christ?

3. If not all the leaders who worked on the U.S. Constitution were Christians and some may have actively despised Christianity as a religion can the Constitution be considered in any sense a Christian document?

4. Who were the prisoners and the oppressed that Jesus came to proclaim liberty for? How did they come to be in bondage? What did freedom mean to such people?

5. Does the slave of Satan have spiritual or emotional liberty? What about the slave of Christ? Is the slave of Christ free to fulfil the ultimate purpose for which he or she was created?

6. Why did the church stop proclaiming liberty to all the spheres of its world? What is the danger of withdrawing into personal spirituality?

7. What does the First Amendment to the U.S. Constitution really mean about church-state relations?

Notebook

The freedom of Christ calls us to a public lifestyle in which we, as the slaves of Christ, proclaim liberty to others. In your notebook make a prayer diary: What persons do you know who need freedom? Note institutions and governments that have left behind Patrick Henry's non-negotiables. Are there places, perhaps at work or in a degraded slum or around a clinic that kills the unborn, where Satan's rule seems unassailable? Pray that the true liberty of Christ's victory might make a difference there.

Chapter 4: A Day Saved for Eternity

Words to define

Sabbath   holy cessation
synagogue   means of grace
worship

Points to ponder

1. From the creation of the world the Sabbath has been a God-ordained blessing for all people.

2. The Sabbath is the keystone for a week-long life cycle of worship and praise.

3. In one day each week of God-centeredness we find that all of life belongs to God, that the pattern is God's to direct, and that the mediator who leads God-centered worship is Jesus Christ.

Questions to answer

1. Why would God have continued the two institutions of the home and the Sabbath after the fall? What did the Sabbath do for a fallen Adam and Eve?

2. If the Sabbath was established on the seventh day of the week, why do Christians celebrate it on the first day? Did this change come from God, and did it enrich the meaning of the Sabbath rest?

3. Why is Sunday worship important to unbelievers, as well as to the saved? Does its loss as a national institution have any ramifications for society and the family in other ways?

4. In what way is Jesus Christ the mediator of worship before God? Which is more important in public worship—communicating with God or communicating with other people?

5. What does Charles Spurgeon's story illustrate about worship within the context of our entire relationship with God?

6. How does one prepare to celebrate the Sabbath? Does it involve actions, thoughts, or both?

7. Does keeping the Sabbath mean refraining from anything that might be fun and enjoyable? Does it mean reserving a day for family fun and relaxation? What does it mean?

Notebook

Look at an order of worship from a recent Sunday service in your church community. Each activity or element should reflect a dialog between God and the group of worshipers or the individual. Note the parts of the service that give God time to communicate in some way with you and others in his body. Note those parts in which the worshipers are communicating praise back to God. Write your own order of worship, choosing songs and Scriptures that demonstrate this divine dialog.

Chapter 5: Sand in the Shoes

Words to define

oaths   one flesh
vows   covenants

Points to ponder

1. How we treat others reflects how we treat God. And in our fallenness we try to weasel out of obligations to others and to God.

2. The sand of devaluing, disinterest, criticism, and unforgiveness adds pain and misery to relationships, but people throw it in one another's shoes anyway because they feel better about themselves when the other person is torn down.

3. Whole relationships start with seeking to lift the value of the other person—looking for whatever is noble, right, pure, lovely, admirable, excellent, and praiseworthy.

Questions to answer

1. Since the Bible closely connects our love for God to our love for others, might our interpersonal relationships be regarded either as acts of worship for God or acts of rebellion against him personally? Why would Jesus demand that we forgive others so that God will forgive us?

2. What does the disintegration of the family in the Roman Empire and in the United States say about the spiritual and emotional dangers faced by Western society at the end of the twentieth century? What are some possible reasons why this disintegration has so rapidly increased since World War II?

3. What are the implications of the Bible's statement that a husband and wife are one flesh? Why does that mean more than considering a marriage a fifty-fifty partnership?

4. Why does forgiveness come so hard for sinful human beings? Why is it sometimes so difficult even to forgive oneself?

5. Is it true that when we label someone they come to be that image? If so, might we not break cycles of despair and failure if we give people the opportunity for respect, instead of a handout?

6. What new dimension can the love of Jesus Christ bring to the process of change in a family? In a church? In a community? In a nation? In a world?

Notebook

The poem at the end of this chapter shows that love in the everyday is a work of building up, encouraging, overlooking, and accepting. Pick out someone close to you in your life—a spouse, a child, a close friend. Write

down the sort of lover you would like to be to that person
and think about what they need most from you. What
can you do to mirror Jesus through your relationship with
that person?

Chapter 6: Holy, Catholic Church

Words to define

koinonia	agent of reconciliation	catholic
Bridegroom	inclusive/exclusive	saints
visible/invisible	communion of saints	holy

Points to ponder

1. Jesus built his church upon the rock of the profession of faith that he is the divine Redeemer, Savior,
and Lord. Churches and believers falter, but Christ's
true church forever prevails.

2. Through Christ's atonement God is reconciling all
creation. That reconciliation preeminently includes
bringing people into God's kingdom under Christ's
headship.

3. The church is an imperfect community, but it is
a community of brothers and sisters and the means by
which God has provided agents of reconciliation to
the world.

Questions to answer

1. The projected growth figures of the church in
the world show a dynamic, growing force. Why is it
we sometimes don't feel the victory in this vast
movement?

2. What is the greatest purpose of the church in the world? How do individuals partake of that great purpose?

3. In what ways is Jesus Christ our high priest? How is the church a partner in the priesthood of Christ, a royal priesthood for the nations of the human race?

4. In what practical ways can you be a parent to every youngster in the congregation you are part of? Is that a responsibility that extends beyond having a Christian education program? Should more be done to encourage everyone in your congregation in this role?

5. People sometimes condemn "organized religion," but should not the church be organized? When does organization in the visible church get in the way of the work of the invisible church in the world?

6. Can the unity of the Holy Spirit overcome ethnic, racial, economic, and cultural boundaries? How can members stimulate this unity among diversity?

7. Can the church be united in Christ while still remaining separated into denominations?

Notebook

The church exists as God intends when each member is tapped and shared for the building up of the others. From this sharing, God's love overflows into the world. Perhaps there are things your church should do or you might become involved in, such as training in personal evangelism, helping young neighborhood parents, serving a nearby school, becoming more aware of moral issues, or taking part in world missions. Think through some creative ideas, possibly the beginning of something that could be presented to the elders and deacons as a new way of being the church.

Chapter 7: "I Will Not Be Shaken"

Words to define

hope	last judgment	resurrection
Alpha and *Omega*	New Jerusalem	transfiguration
eschatology	intermediate state	

Points to ponder

1. The Christian's hope is a confidence we now know a view of eternity we do not have to wait to see.

2. The future state of the Christian will be in the presence of God's glory in a renewed body, a renewed worship, a renewed society, and a renewed identification with Christ.

3. What God wants us to know about the end of history is that it is coming and we need to be ready for it.

Questions to answer

1. Why do you think the Bible offers an incomplete picture of what heaven will be like and when Christ will return? Wouldn't we be better off having all the answers?

2. What does it mean to live transcendently? How does someone with this attitude cope with sickness or tragedy? What does transcendent living have to do with righteousness?

3. Why does our generation experience so much hopelessness and fearfulness at a time of great technological and informational advances?

4. What benefits do believers receive from Christ at death? Are blessings suggested by the *Westminster Confession* for the body as well as the soul?

5. Does it seem odd to think that heaven will have no churches? What will take their place in the worship of God? Is there any sense in which that heavenly kind of worship can take place now, on earth?

6. How can anyone stand unshaken before God in his day of judgment?

7. What did Paul do in times of beatings, danger, and imprisonment? Was he ever down emotionally? Why wasn't his faith shaken in the dark night of the soul? What should the Christian do in times of doubt and depression?

Notebook

Do a self-inventory, honestly looking at the state of your relationship with Christ. Are you to the point where you cannot be shaken, no matter what happens? What have you done in the last week that has eternal significance—what would not burn away in the day of testing by God's fire? Remember that these eternally valuable building materials are those that serve your purpose to glorify God and enjoy him forever.

Chapter 8: Transforming Truths

Questions about the *Westminster Confession of Faith* and *Catechisms*

1. When the *Shorter Catechism* answers the question concerning the "chief end of man," what is being said about the central theme and focus of life? What is the alternative to this focus?

2. In the *Larger Catechism*'s statement of proofs that the Scriptures are the Word of God, which proofs come from the Bible itself? Are any of these proofs sufficient to persuade the sinful person of the Bible's truth? What proof is sufficient?

3. What facts about God as Triune do the Westminster catechisms draw from Scripture?

4. Why can the purposes of God be called "eternal"? Is it troubling to say that God has ordained for his own glory everything that comes to pass?

5. What was the nature of the first sin? Why was it unforgiveable? Is that one sin ultimately responsible for all subsequent sins, and if so, why would God allow it to happen?

6. What does the Bible mean when it says that all are by nature children of wrath? How does that wrath show itself?

7. What was the significance for us when God unveiled his covenant of grace after the fall? What was his part of the promise? What was the human part of the promise?

8. What does the *Larger Catechism* mean when it says that the covenant of grace was "administered" in one way under the Old Testament and in another way under the New Testament? What changed?

9. Why did the Mediator have to be both God and human? How could he escape the human condition of sin?

10. Why, according to the *Larger Catechism,* is effectual calling central to union with Christ?

11. Why are justification and adoption called "acts" of God's free grace, and sanctification is called a "work" of God's free grace?

12. According to the *Larger Catechism* questions 85–86, what do we have in death that we could never have in life? What will we lose, at least for a time?

13. What is the difference between the visible and invisible church? Which would be the more important in God's sight?

14. Why is assurance of salvation a problem? Is it a problem that that can be resolved?

15. What is significant about the rejoining of the body and the soul in the resurrection? What will make that new body fundamentally different than it is now?

16. Is there more to the Ten Commandments than a set of rules? What is the underlying principle of each commandment?